RETHINKING EXCESSIVE HABITS AND ADDICTIVE BEHAVIORS

RETHINKING EXCESSIVE HABITS AND ADDICTIVE BEHAVIORS

Tony Bevacqua

ROWMAN & LITTLEFIELD
Lanham • Boulder • New York • London

Published by Rowman & Littlefield
A wholly owned subsidary of The Rowman & Littlefield Publishing Group,
Inc.
4501 Forbes Boulevard, Suite 200, Lanham, Maryland 20706
www.rowman.com

Unit A, Whitacre Mews, 26-34 Stannary Street, London SE11 4AB

British Library Cataloguing in Publication Information Available

Library of Congress Cataloging-in-Publication Data

Bevacqua, Tony.
Rethinking excessive habits and addictive behaviors / Tony Bevacqua.
pages cm
Includes bibliographical references and index.
ISBN 978-1-4422-4829-8 (cloth : alk. paper) -- ISBN 978-1-4422-4830-4 (electronic)
1. Compulsive behavior. 2. Substance abuse. I. Title.
RC533.B48 2015
616.85'84--dc23
2015000014

♾ ™ The paper used in this publication meets the minimum requirements of
American National Standard for Information Sciences Permanence of Paper
for Printed Library Materials, ANSI/NISO Z39.48-1992.

Printed in the United States of America

CONTENTS

131822

FOREWORD

The field of addictive treatment has been stagnant for far too long. Though Alcoholics Anonymous (AA) arose in the 1930s to offer hope and inspiration to those suffering from alcohol dependency, the organization has become more of an obstacle than a beacon over the following decades. AA's core concepts of individual powerlessness and addiction as an inevitably incurable and lifelong "disease" are detrimental to personality growth and change. So too is AA's treatment that encourages individuals with alcohol dependency to focus exclusively on abstinence only without enhancing their need for subjective well-being. Certainly, the specialties of both humanistic and positive psychology in which I've been an active scholar for thirty years have presented alternative ways of viewing alcohol-related problems.

Nevertheless, for important sociohistorical reasons, AA's ideology has not only been essentially unchallenged for many decades, but has even increased its influence through countless twelve-step programs. Though such programs have been lampooned in comedic books, television shows, and movies ("Hi, my name is Al and I'm an alcoholic"), the AA ideology and treatment approach remains hugely influential. This influence is not merely intellectual: It dominates clinics, hospitals, psychotherapy offices, and rehab centers throughout the United States. Even our country's judicial system accepts this ideology unquestioningly if not enthusiastically.

Of course, professional critics exist. But they tend to be few and far between—and generally either academicians or journalists. One of these exceptions is Tony Bevacqua, a Los Angeles-based personal and corporate coach and college psychology instructor whom I've known professionally for the past five years. We first became acquainted through my biography of Abraham Maslow and related articles in various journals.

Though I was aware from my own experience as a clinical psychologist that addiction treatment based on the AA's twelve-step model was dismally ineffective, Tony Bevacqua helped me to see exactly why. As a result of our many phone conversations and e-mail exchanges spanning the continental United States, we decided to collaborate on an article tracing the historical roots of this influential model—and which was subsequently published in the *Journal of Humanistic Psychology.*

Since then, I've been aware of Tony Bevacqua's continuing efforts to explicate the conceptual and treatment deficiencies of the twelve-step approach—and to help promulgate a more effective way of helping the millions of men and women struggling today to overcome their debilitating addictions. I recently learned that he had completed his long-term goal of writing a book on the themes about which he's been lecturing ardently for several years—and was honored to write this foreword. Articulated clearly and forcefully, this book provides a much-needed message for both professionals in this field and lay individuals eager for a fresh perspective.

Particularly interesting to me is Tony Bevacqua's usage of behavioral principles based on Albert Bandura's seminal work known as social learning theory, in addition to incorporating insights on personality development based on psychoanalytic-derived and humanistic concepts. By successfully integrating these seemingly disparate viewpoints, this book breaks new, important psychological ground in understanding and treating addictive disorders.

In this light, a personal anecdote is relevant. When I interviewed B. F. Skinner at his home in the 1980s in conjunction with my biography of Abraham Maslow, I was surprised to hear the world-renowned behaviorist say that he shared Maslow's stirring values about personality growth but simply felt the imperative to ground them in more scientifically rigorous terms.

Trained as an undergraduate at Cornell University to see Maslow and Skinner as psychological archenemies, I found this comment both startling and perplexing. But thanks to this compelling book on addictive behavior and its amelioration, I now clearly see how such a synthesis is not only possible but indeed necessary. It should open a pathway that will finally allow professionals, as well as the concerned lay public, to advance effectively in this domain.

Edward Hoffman, PhD
New York, New York

PREFACE

This book is the culmination of many years of personal and professional experiences. I was born and raised in Fulton, New York, a small factory town at the time. My father worked at the post office and my mother was a teacher's aide. She volunteered to work with both intellectually disabled children and elderly homebound women, and she also tutored children whose primary language was not English. She had a lot of patience and a good heart. Both my parents were all about honor and hard work. They valued work—even the most menial jobs—and combined an authoritarian parenting style with very soft sides. In retrospect, it was my first experience involving cognitive dissonance. My three older siblings were also influential. They all had graduate degrees, worked in education fields, and had completely different ways than my parents of looking at the world. I attended Catholic parochial school and served as an altar boy for a while, at both weddings and funerals. Such experiences of duality—watching people with so much happiness as well as those with intense sorrow—helped me develop empathy and compassion at an early age.

Later, while studying graduate psychology at Pepperdine University, I was further influenced by some of my courses. In my first graduate class, one professor handed out two books that made a big impression on me—the first on critical thinking and the other essentially about questioning everything they were teaching. I thought this was very open-minded, and it enlarged my perspective about learning in general.

When I first entered the field of addiction treatment, I found it disturbing. I saw many people seriously challenged with their own problems involving drugs and alcohol—barely keeping their own lives in order—yet freely dispensing advice to newly vulnerable, suffering men and women. That dynamic seemed counterintuitive, especially when these counselors asserted their opinions with so much self-assured certainty. I saw very little self-discovery occurring during treatment sessions, as well as little attempt to help clients understand themselves and learn to cope better with life. If they did not immediately accept what they were being told, they were pejoratively labeled as "noncompliant." I did not witness much compassion or empathy. I increasingly felt that the language being used was too deficit-based, emotionally charged, and carrying too many negative connotations..

In this light, several anecdotes readily come to mind, and I'd like to share three in particular. Roy (not his real name) was a sixty-three-year-old highly functional married man and homeowner. He was also a habitual wine drinker, and one night while driving home, he received a DUI. Roy was court-mandated to attend both Alcoholic Anonymous (AA) meetings and outpatient counseling. Roy recounted that in his first AA meeting, the group leader rambled on about his terrible childhood, his explosive anger problem, and his current problematic family life—as others in the room all nodded in acknowledgment. He then forcefully began to tell newcomers what they needed to do to help themselves with their "disease" of alcohol dependency. Roy commented to me, "Why would I ever listen to someone for advice whose own life was clearly a mess? I got up and walked out."

I reasoned that Roy's pattern of drinking wine and then driving was a bad decision—inconsiderate, potentially dangerous, and not smart. But was it a disease? After one coaching session with me, Roy successfully went about his life. And the AA approach to addictive behaviors increasingly seemed overly simplistic to me.

Around the same time, I was working at an outpatient drug counseling center in Los Angeles. One afternoon, no fewer than ten staff members were having a case conference about a client—let's call him Jorge: a middle-aged, Hispanic man who was court-mandated for treatment because of his arrest for disorderly conduct. He had been drinking heavily and causing problems by loitering and using abusive language. My coworkers remarked that Jorge often came intoxicated to our facility, never passed his urine testing, and angrily rebuffed efforts of professional help. Nobody wanted to work with him. I volunteered to take him on. Prior to my involvement, Jorge had undergone two years of mostly confrontational counseling involving staff members who experienced counter-transference regularly because of their own negative experiences with drugs and alcohol. They remained frustrated and took Jorge's refusal to cooperate as a personal insult.

After eight weeks of working with me, Jorge started to enjoy better subjective experiences. How so? Because I did not tell him to stop drinking. I did not confront him with my perceived absolute belief that I knew what he needed to do for himself. Because I was humanistic in my approach and only tangentially discussed his drinking behavior through much of our hourly sessions, Jorge began to cut back his alcohol consumption on his own, find a job, exercise more often, and ultimately reconnect with his estranged wife. At our facility, Jorge gradually became pleasant and friendly—and showed behavioral change that appeared to be organic and not forced.

Finally, Alice (not her real name) was a young homeless woman who had been arrested for drug possession. Diagnosed as schizophrenic (perhaps erroneously), she was a client who had also been passed around from one counselor to another. Nobody seemed able to work with Alice effectively because of her erratic behavior and apparent delusions. Like Jorge, she had been unable to pass random drug tests. She also smelled awful. She had been coming for about a year.

I offered to see Alice. I allowed her to act as she wanted. I acknowledged her presence respectfully and asked her questions about her imagined life. Over time, Alice came in with greater cleanliness and began passing her random drug tests. After months of mostly irrational conversations, I vividly recall, she sat down with me one morning. In an essentially normal voice (that almost suggested to me that her entire past behavior had been a performance), Alice remarked that she liked coming to see me because I was the only person who had ever listened to her. This seemingly incurable, homeless, and delusional woman "cleaned up her act" shortly thereafter. I had always felt that Alice had real strengths—survival skills that enabled her to live on the streets. If she could accomplish that, she could also take control of her life in these other areas that were becoming a problem. That was my belief, and it proved accurate.

Besides my work in the addiction field, I am a college instructor in psychology. For me, teaching is a microcosm for life. I am committed to diversity. Each semester, I require that my students write their auto-biographies. In doing so, they demonstrate that while they may not be familiar with the abstract language of psychology, they do in fact live it every day. Despite their difficult lives, many are incredibly resilient. Therefore, one of my primary goals, besides my educational objectives, is to empower students to grow and change in all aspects of their lives. These writing assignments reveal difficult life experiences that are dominated directly or indirectly by mental health and substance-related issues. In my view, these issues directly affect their motivation, hopes, dreams, aspirations, self-esteem, identity, and effort.

As true for my coaching work involving people with addictive behaviors, I regard each college student as a unique individual—and I seek to be empathetic to a student's particular circumstances. Having worked professionally for over a decade with people challenged by their bad habits and addictive behaviors, I have discovered that the underlying theme for most is that they feel powerless and hopeless at the start. But I empower, challenge, and help them to change the ways they think about themselves. I have found that teaching that way is very effective as well. Within the first few weeks every semester, I learn each student's name and something unique about that particular person. In other words, I see people as self-empowering human beings *first*—and only *second*, as possessing particular life challenges that may include addictive disorders.

If this book succeeds in conveying this viewpoint based on relevant psychological theories and my own hard-earned experiences as a counselor and coach, it will have fulfilled its purpose.

INTRODUCTION

Does our genetic composition dictate or control our behavior? This is a key question at the outset, and recent thinkers say the answer is definitely *no*. In *Wired for Culture: Origins of the Human Social Mind*, evolutionary biologist Mark Pagel contends that culture is the driving force of change in human history. In other words, culture has exerted more impact than genes on human civilization. In Pagel's cogent view, social learning has created culture and language has a subversive power, too.[1] How so? Because social conformity is powerfully enforced through language. For example, when our behaviors produce feelings of *guilt* and *shame*, these words induce—as Sigmund Freud would say— an intrapsychic discontent. Similarly, words like *compassion* and *empathy*, learned and expressed, generate different feelings involving intrapsychic contentment.

Writing from a somewhat different perspective in *Mean Genes*, Terry Burnham and Jay Phalen assert that, "Our temptations are powerful and persistent, but we are not destined to succumb."[2] They suggest that even if our biological cravings for food or sex are attributable to genetic predisposition, we're also genetically predisposed to making conscious behavioral choices. Thus, both psychological and biological phenomena complement each other—rather than cause cognition, emotions, and behavior to occur as separate realities.

In my view, the current enthusiasm over brain science in attempting to explain the causal basis of addictive behavior is therefore misguided. It involves reductionist thinking and has little utility. Such thinking not only devalues psychological phenomena, but minimizes the importance of cultural, environmental, and social realities.

Let's take the example of depression. A psychological explanation would say that people suffering from this condition have challenging life problems for which they lack adequate coping skills—or unresolved emotional issues like early abuse, trauma, or low self-esteem. The goal is to change his/her conscious thinking through talk therapy in a way that will alleviate the severity of his/her negative moods. In this process, communication between the therapist and the client is always mediated by how each has framed their view of reality.

From a biological viewpoint, the depressed individual has a chemical imbalance—and by the administering of prescribed drugs, the balance will be restored and the negative mood will be stabilized. When either approach appears to be effective, it's touted as "proof" of its efficacy. Psychotherapy claims that the individual's personality has now been improved and pharmaceutical intervention claims that something physical within the brain has now been corrected. Yet, neither intervention, however seemingly successful, *proves* cause and effect.

Why? Because taken either separately or together, these two perspectives involve two separate realities about human behavior. At best, such a dualistic approach to behavior has only limited usefulness because it's reductionist. Indeed, in my view, this dualism actually complicates our attempt to understand addictive behavior and therefore maintains it, rather than shedding light and advancing our professional perspective.

For example, look at the current thinking used in mainstream conceptualization, definition, and treatment approaches to addictive behaviors. First, for the ostensible purpose of diagnostic and treatment standardization, addiction has essentially been medicalized. Advocates for this development claim this is progress, but it's ultimately only the imposition of a socially constructed perception of reality. How do I mean? Simply that politics and science are brought together to sustain a particular agenda: determining how the brain affects the symptoms associated with addictive behavior. Popularly depicted by mass media as absolute truth, such studies involving dopamine sensitivity and dopamine receptors (the brain's "reward" area), seemingly provide a biological explanation for addictive behavior. Distressed individuals are then told by most treatment professionals they have a "disease" like diabetes or cancer. Unfortunately, because of cultural indoctrination, few understand that the word "disease" in this context is not literal.

Despite over forty years of research on addictive behavior, no conclusive evidence exists for an addiction gene, a bodily allergy, or a chemical imbalance—or even that such behavior is significantly related to a particular genetic inheritance. Yet, mainstream thinking mandates that these individuals—who have been labeled as having a disease (actually, nothing more than a socially constructed biological explanation) participate in support groups insisting that the cause of their disease is something spiritual and other-worldly (a socially constructed psychological-transcendental explanation). These are two quite different perceptions of realities simultaneously presented as absolute truths.

Moreover, both approaches lack something vital: the individual's own viewpoint—how reality is framed based upon personal experience involving language. In my view, almost all human reality is preceded by language and communication. Everything we communicate is an expression of our subjectivity: that is, how we experience ourselves in the world. Having full command and authority over our self-determining nature is tremendously self-empowering.

Why has the problem of addictive behavior remained relatively unchanged decade after decade, despite new evidence-based treatments and medical interventions? Because by separating the mind and the body (brain), and treating this problem from two quite polarizing perspectives, therapeutic efforts remain ensnared by outdated strategies—not at all congruent with today's reality. For example, *The Big Book* of Alcoholics Anonymous (AA) was written in 1939, yet it's still the unquestioned basis for the numerous twelve-step programs that have emerged from AA. Indeed, *The Big Book*'s first 164 pages are virtually unchanged since first published. What was presented initially as a means to alleviate alcoholic drinking in the Great Depression era when little was known about this condition is *still* the dominant viewpoint seventy-six years later!

This situation itself is illogical enough, but at the same time, when technological advances are now occurring almost daily, the most sophisticated brain science coexists in mainstream addiction treatment with this scientifically outdated thinking. The two approaches are logically incompatible. For example, it would be illogical to suggest to exercise daily, and when finished, smoke a cigarette. If healthcare industry experts really believed that support groups were vital to treat medical conditions (mental health has already been medicalized), then why aren't cancer patients told they're powerless, need to seek a higher power, get a sponsor, and attend group meetings for effective treatment?

Let's examine the dualistic effect on maintaining substance dependency when language like a dual-diagnosis is employed. A person with a drinking problem and who is experiencing depression is said to have both of these conditions co-occurring. The dominant professional recommendation for treatment would be to attend AA meetings indefinitely and to take antidepressants for the foreseeable future. For both types of intervention, this individual is encouraged to think: "If I ever stop attending meetings, I'm likely to start drinking again" and "If don't take antidepressants every day, my depression will return."

But what is this person actually experiencing when feeling depressed and by consuming too much alcohol? Might the depression have preceded the additive behaviors? Neither condition is literally a disease. Typically, antidepressants are replaced with different ones until the desired outcome is reached. But what *is* the desired outcome? Is it positive well-being? No.

In both instances, such dual-diagnosed people are hampered by their inability to broaden their narrow frame of thinking. Moreover, they are persuaded by mainstream professionals to accept as absolute truth two highly opposing conceptions of their problem. Yet neither approach is accurate, for neither their depression nor their drinking is really a disease.

Another example of insufficient critical thinking in the addiction treatment field concerns the supposedly scientific claim that drugs like heroin exert long-term effects that structurally alter the brain. Yet, the primary treatment for heroin abuse today is to replace heroin with another opiate drug like methadone for long-term usage. Well, what happens now to the brain? Isn't it structurally changing too? Oddly enough, almost nobody talks about this.

It's a truism to say that subjectivity is what separates human beings from other animals. Science can study the nervous system of animals and generalize findings to human conditions. Science can use brain imaging to peer into maladaptive brains and make interpretations that will also be generalized. But we can never generalize personal experiences in the same manner. Our thoughts, beliefs, feelings—and more importantly, how we have learned to frame our perception of reality in every moment of our lives is what makes us unique as humans. Of course, we're all part of humanity and we're all part of the human condition. But our experience of reality is exclusively individualistic. For nobody can know what's happening this moment inside our brain on a molecular level.

By deconstructing the rampant dualism in the addiction field, we can free ourselves from the deficit-based language that has indoctrinated us to accept a narrow view of reality and kept us stuck. Think of the mind as a metaphor for a lifetime of stored experiences. Addictive behaviors provide a wonderful opportunity for us to change, grow, and live to our fullest potential.

Words are very persuasive. They dictate our understanding of ourselves and others. Words give us the reference points derived from our own experiences to bond with others in ways that seem comfortable and familiar. But we have to see individualist experience as ultimately unique. You might have a problem similar to someone else, but it's never identical because you have your own subjective experience. For this reason, I avoid the word "addiction" because it's an emotionally charged word that generates images of worst-case alcoholics and drug addicts—who are atypical of most men and women.

I don't believe anyone is powerless or diseased. Thus, I'm advocating a reappraisal of the conceptual language and terminology used in this field—key elements which have become mere buzzwords utilized to standardize how the system operates. In the same way that theories are used to help explain various psychological phenomena—and some theories are more useful than others—I believe the more useful approach to conceptualizing the issue of addictive behavior is to deconstruct the dualistic separation of psychological and biological perceived realities. Why not create a new conceptual language, in which the mind/brain connection is actually simply mind/brain living system?

Cognitive and emotional responses aren't reducible to a particular neural network because these networks are always changing. As psychologist Louis Cozolino states, "the brain is neither predetermined nor unchanging, but rather is an organ of adaptation."[3] Because humans are unique individuals, changes in neural networks in different people at different times will show up as different psychological experiences.

Therefore a more useful conceptualization of addictive behavior (or any behavior) is that an individual's subjective experience (a psychological phenomenon) affects both psychological and biological responses.

Of course, the implications of deconstructing dualism would necessitate quite a conceptual shift concerning cognitive and emotional behavior. Think about the conventional approach to treating addictive behaviors. Listen to the language used to socially conform someone to the acceptance of the condition. "Abstinence only" is reductionist thinking. "Relapse equates with failure." Again, reductionist thinking. The disease label implies more reductionist thinking.

How much power and influence for change and positive well-being would result if professionals refrained from declaring with absolute certainty that a person was an alcoholic, had a disease and was powerless, and instead said that the individual is human, challenged by life circumstances, and can creatively change the quality of their thinking?

Language serves many functions. It's used to describe events, situations, and people. But communication always needs to be collaborative. In *Tools for Critical Thinking: Metathoughts for Psychology*, David Levy argues that there's an evaluative bias in language. "The words that we use can, with or without our intent, become powerful instruments of change. In those instances where we are deliberately attempting to influence others to agree with our point of view, we intentionally select words that most persuasively communicate our values. We should therefore, not present our value judgments as objective reflections of truth, and that value judgments inherent in other people's use of language, in many cases tells us at least as much about them as the events and individuals they are attempting to describe."[4]

To change human behavior, we must change our language.

And this principle certainly applies to discourse about addictive behaviors. For millennia, people have been communicating and disseminating knowledge and information through storytelling. The stories which play out daily in the mass media today are just that: stories that one can choose to interpret subjectively. For the "news"—which is purportedly objective, is actually subjective as well—because it's always reported from the framework of personal viewpoints.

Storytelling is powerful because words and language are powerful. Since prehistory, shamans in diverse cultures have used stories to heal suffering and confusion. The appeal is universal. The popularity of fairy tales like *Snow White* transcends age, race, ethnicity, and cultural differences. Historically, the head of the family would tell the same stories over and over, but there would always be something a little different added or subtracted. People write and rewrite the stories of themselves, and these new stories hold the potential for new ways of experiencing our lives and ourselves. "In editing our narratives we change the organization and nature of our memories and hence, reorganize our brains as well as our minds."[5]

Let's take the common example of a boy who is exhibiting difficulties at school. The focus is placed on his observable behavior and the interpretations made by his teachers and parents. They communicate that the behavior is inappropriate and a problem that needs to be treated. And so, the boy becomes the problem. However, by allowing his story also to be integrated into the process of meaning-making, family members come to understand that they all contribute to the issue. By reframing their thinking, the family and teacher may decide that perhaps nothing is wrong with the boy's behavior—and neither drugs nor alarm is necessary. Thus, we begin to see the use of individual stories in providing the basis for better communication—and the appropriate basis for change and problem-solving. Otherwise, we reduce the behavior to biology and prescribe drugs to deal with it.

People have expertise concerning their own lives and can become primary authors of the stories they tell themselves about themselves. This narrative is therefore the primary component of their experience and their language is the structured means to communicate it.

In his latest book, *Recover!*, Stanton Peele, who for decades has been at the forefront of challenging the thinking and language used in the addiction industry, offers a humane description of addictive behavior. He asserts, "Addiction is the search for a sense of security, a sense of being loved, even a sense of control over life. But, gratification is temporary and illusory, and the behavioral results instead in greater self-disgust, reduced psychological security and poorer coping ability. That's what all addictions have in common."[6]

Outside of his use of the emotionally charged word "addiction" Peele's description really addresses the human condition and he views the problem compassionately and empathically. This is not the language of mainstream thinking. For me, addictive behaviors result when an individual—despite biology, cognition, emotions, and social conditioning—willfully resists the necessary courage needed for creative control over their subjectivity to negotiate their real and perceived realities.

Conventional ways of dealing with addictive behaviors are part of the problem and not the solution. Why? Because the solution is in the creative thinking that empowers the individual to reframe the reductionism that was inherited through both biology and social conditioning.

Let's take a practical example. Your relationship with your spouse is causing you a great deal of stress. This is the practical reality. The reason for this reality has something to do with the quality of your communication with your spouse. The quality of your communication is directly affected by how you frame your subjectivity—that is, everything you think, feel, and believe about yourself and your spouse and people in general.

Based on your coping skills or lack thereof, you have a choice to make on how to deal with the stress caused by the relationship. You can choose to get drunk to temporarily remove and avoid the unpleasant feeling of discontent, or you can expand your thinking by rethinking: thinking more and thinking often. When you think better, you'll communicate better. When you communicate better, you're more likely to address the realities of the relationship problems. Instead of consuming alcohol to relieve stress, you'll rely upon the coping skills of active listening, problem solving, and conflict resolution. Of course, some people choose to remain stuck by staying in old patterns out of the need for comfort and familiarity, or fear of change. But that's a choice, not a disease.

To change behavior, we must change our language. Language precedes behavior. We "hear" others talking, but it doesn't necessarily register as authentic because we use the more primitive areas of our brain to react automatically from learning that's stored unconsciously. It's through becoming a better "listener" that a person can become more generous and authentic because they're less distracted by the chatter within their own head.

In *Power of Mindful Learning*, Ellen Langer describes the importance of making the conscious choice to dwell in the moment to notice the context of things in our world. In her view, a *mindful* person is open to new information and creates new ways of looking at things. One becomes aware that other perspectives exist. Certainly, a big reason why many people are stressfully stuck in their subjectivity is because they're fearful. Fear induces us to seek certainty—and this dysfunctional process is usually learned in childhood.

Langer contends that since there is no certainty because everything changes in the real world, one who gravitates toward the need for certainty is led to *mindlessness*: remaining stuck in old ways of thinking and automatic behaviors.[7] I would maintain that this mindlessness is the foundation of how addictive behavior develops and manifests.

For people who have chosen and learned to use addictive behaviors to cope with their life challenges, they need to change the experience of themselves which has been shaped and formed by culture and language. This autonomy in thinking will provide them the freedom and flexibility to make new choices and evolve as human beings.

To sum it up, fear and the need for certainty invariably inhibit human growth. A change in language and in the quality of thinking will therefore benefit anyone who is experiencing concerns or consequences either directly or indirectly related to their addictive behavior because it will empower them to be less mindless and more mindful.

1

THE ORIGINS OF THE AA MINDSET

Before revisioning the contemporary field of addiction treatment, it's important to understand how we arrived at this point. Alcoholics Anonymous (AA), and the numerous twelve-step programs it has spawned, did not arise out of a vacuum. Rather, its intelligent and dedicated founders came to their outlook through specific historical-cultural forces. In this context, the philosophical impact of one particular thinker, William James, is key to learning its history. Over the course of his lifetime, he influenced a host of academic disciplines within the United States and abroad. Generally regarded as America's greatest philosopher, he also founded its psychology field. Because James's interest rests in the heights of human personality and its untapped potential, he can well be viewed as a grandparent of both humanistic and positive psychology.

However, James has undoubtedly been most influential within the United States through his intellectual linkage to AA, founded twenty-five years after his death in 1910—and more broadly, to the entire addiction recovery movement known today as twelve-step programs. That is, by emphasizing James's concept of self-surrender during intense despair—similar to what Abraham Maslow later called the *nadir experience*—AA developed a "one-size-fits-all" model of addiction recovery that has essentially excluded all other approaches. Such a situation evolved from the nadir experience of AA's founder Bill Wilson, and subsequently became AA's sole paradigm for addiction recovery. Ironically, James never intended his observations about what he called the "sick-minded soul" and self-surrender to be a universal model for alcoholism recovery, but wisely recommended a pluralistic perspective that emphasized the diversity of human temperaments.

WILLIAM JAMES AND ALCOHOL DEPENDENCY

As a psychologist, James is known for his insights on numerous subjects, though alcohol dependency is not typically among these. Yet, he discussed alcoholism (or *dipsomania*, as it was then called in the medical field) frequently in his psychological writings. Having received his medical degree from Harvard in 1869, he was undoubtedly aware that alcohol dependency had been regarded as a disease for more than half a century. The medical term *dipsomania* (taken from the Greek "thirst frenzy") had been introduced by Dr. Wilhelm C. Hufeland of Prussia in 1819 in his preface to *Trunksucht* (Dipsomania), a pioneering study of the phenomenon by C. von Bruhl-Cramer, a German-Russian physician. Two years earlier the Italian physician Salvatori had been the first to identify "the habit of drinking in an excessive manner of wine and strong drink, and of a special disease the offspring of it."[1]

Nor is it difficult to ascertain the origin of James's personal interest in alcohol dependency, for several of his closest family members struggled bitterly with this condition. Those afflicted with alcoholism included his wealthy erudite father, his younger brother Robertson, and his father-in-law, Daniel Gibbens. Though William James's father seemed to have cured himself in midlife of alcohol dependency, Robertson James eventually died from an alcohol-related disease, and physician Daniel Gibbens committed suicide after years of struggling with alcoholism. Such was the tragic impact of alcohol dependency in William James's own family.

How did James actually view alcoholism? In *Principles of Psychology*—on which he labored for a decade until its publication in 1890—James (1890/1981) declared that "the love of drunkenness is a purely accidental susceptibility of a brain . . . and its causes are to be sought out in a molecular realm, rather than in any possible order of 'outer relations.'"[2] In this landmark text, James offered many anecdotes to show the strength of the addictive power of liquor for dipsomaniacs, including the horrific account of an institutionalized man who had intentionally chopped off one of his hands to obtain rum to medically bathe his resulting "stump" and thereby snatch some rum to drink. The man was so addicted, he intentionally cut his hand off because he knew the injury would be treated with alcohol that he would proceed to drink as well. Perhaps thinking of his own brother Robertson, James in *Principles* described the many rationalizations that dipsomaniacs offered in relapsing, and argued that such rationalizations were merely an evasion about the truth of their condition. Several years after *Principles* was published to wide acclaim, James agreed to lecture at the Harvard Total Abstinence League, an anti-alcohol student organization. He was familiar with the group, having addressed it favorably when founded in 1888.

Thus, in January 1895, James reviewed for his audience the physiology of alcohol consumption and offered several stark conclusions. Though admitting that he occasionally drank liquor, James insisted that "to work on alcohol is a most treacherous business, even where it does stimulate, if it does. In most cases, it merely masks the fatigue and makes the matter worse. . . . The whole bill against alcohol is its treachery. Its happiness is an illusion and seven other demons return."[3]

Unquestionably, James's most influential view of alcohol dependency came from his 1901–1902 Edinburgh lecture series on *The Varieties of Religious Experience.* James did not devote any of his twenty lectures specifically to the topic, but presented his view indirectly—particularly in detailing the "conversion" experience of Samuel Hadley. A chronic abuser of alcohol, Hadley was close to forty years old and homeless in New York City, when one night in 1882 his despair reached suicidal level. Ready to drown himself, Hadley suddenly felt a "great and mighty presence" and instantly vowed never to touch a drop of liquor again.[4] Later in the week, he sought out the Jerry McCauley Mission in the Bowery, and amidst McCauley's fervent group prayer, Hadley affirmed Jesus as his savior. "From that moment until now, I have never wanted another drink of whiskey," Hadley later wrote, "and I have never seen money enough to make me take one."[5]

Within a few weeks, Hadley had completely straightened out his chaotic life, and eventually became the well-respected director of the Bowery Mission that had welcomed him as a forlorn vagrant. Indeed, the same year that *Varieties* was published, Hadley's memoir was also published, chronicling his sixteen years in alcoholism recovery. More than a decade after Hadley's death in 1906, his career was recapped in an inspirational book, *Christian Standards in Life*, aimed at Christian college students.

For James, episodes like Hadley's were living proof that even the most severe cases of alcohol dependency were potentially curable through "conversion"—what today's humanistic psychologists might call self-transformation. In James's influential view, conversion involves the "process, gradual or sudden, by which a self, hereto divided and consciously wrong, inferior, and unhappy, becomes unified and consciously right, superior, and happy."[6] In citing the findings of several contemporary researchers, James contended that conversion typically depended on two psychological conditions: (1) an outlook of "brooding, depression, and morbid introspection" and (2) a sense of powerlessness that leads to self-surrender.[7]

It is important to note that James affirmed that some types of conversion may instead involve qualities like joyful inspiration, pleasure, and volition, but he asserted that these "as a rule [are] *less interesting* than those of the self-surrender type."[8] More broadly, James viewed conversion as a phenomenon most connected to what he called the "sick-minded soul" or "morbid-minded soul"—that is, an individual who views the world darkly and filled with evil. James contrasted this outlook with what he called the "healthy-minded" perspective, which is essentially optimistic.

It is clear that James sought to be as objective as possible in differentiating "healthy-minded" versus "morbid" sensibilities. Throughout his lecture titled *The Sick Soul*, he differentiated the "sanguine" and "sunny" perspective from the "depressed and melancholy," suggesting that these emanated from inborn disposition rather than life experience. For instance, James noted that, "[Some] are born close to the pain-threshold, which the slightest irritants fatally send them over [the misery line]."[9]

In the same lecture, James speculated whether different "sort[s] of religion" might be necessary for people with differing dispositions toward life—a brilliant idea that remains unrealized more than a century later. James returned to this crucial viewpoint in his final lecture titled *Conclusions*. Rhetorically raising the question, "Ought it be assumed that the lives of all men should show identical religious elements?" He declared:

I answer "No!" emphatically. And my reason is that I do not see it possible that creatures in such different positions and with such different powers as human individuals are, should have exactly the same functions and the same duties. No two of us have the same identical difficulties, nor should we be expected to work out identical solutions. Each, from his particular angle of observation, takes in a certain sphere of fact and trouble, which each must deal with in a unique manner. One of us must soften himself, another must harden himself; one must yield a point, another must stand firm in order to better defend the position assigned to him. . . . Individuals must be allowed to get [to a union with the divine] by the channels which lie most open to their several temperaments. [10]

JAMES, THE OXFORD GROUP, AND THE FOUNDING OF AA

James died less than a year after meeting Freud and Jung at Clark University in 1909, but his writings continued to inspire social scientists and philosophers. With its emphasis on religious experience as a positive force in human life, his *Varieties* particularly appealed to educated clergy. Among these was Frank Buchman, a Lutheran minister from Pennsylvania who founded in the early 1930s what became popularly known as the Oxford Group. An offshoot of the First Century Christian Fellowship that Buchman had established on college campuses throughout the United States a decade earlier, the Oxford Group was centered on Buchman's vigorous proselytizing efforts in Oxford, England, and espoused humanity's redemption through individual moral regeneration. Buchman emphasized "four absolutes" as keys in this process: "absolute honesty, absolute purity, absolute unselfishness, and absolute love."

Buchman had not created the Oxford Group specifically for people struggling with alcohol dependency. Rather, his protégé, Dr. Samuel Shoemaker—rector of New York City's Episcopal Calvary Church—was most directly responsible for refining and sharing the Oxford Group's message for such people. The two clergy had first met as Protestant missionaries in China back in 1917. Shoemaker was a prolific writer, who, from his first book, *Realizing Religion*, published in 1921, was enamored with William James's work.

Shoemaker repeatedly quoted James and stated, for example, "If you want a comprehensive scientific definition of conversion, William James has given us a good one: 'The process, gradual or sudden, by which a self, hitherto divided and consciously wrong, inferior and unhappy, becomes unified, consciously right, superior, and happy.'"[11] Shoemaker was also a better thinker than Buchman, who while engaged in proselytizing work in Nazi Germany, established friendly ties with Nazi Party leaders.

The Oxford Group would eventually self-destruct under Buchman's pro-Nazi sentiments. However, they were initially viewed favorably by many Americans struggling with alcohol dependency. Among these were several acquaintances of an unemployed Wall Street stockbroker suffering from chronic and worsening alcohol dependency, William "Bill" Wilson. It would be no exaggeration to say that Wilson, who would quickly emerge as AA's main founder and promoter, would become James's greatest popularizer and distorter.

Born in rural Vermont in 1895, Wilson was abandoned by both his parents following their divorce when he was ten years old. His hard-drinking father headed north for Canada and his mother moved to Boston, leaving the sickly child to live with his maternal grandparents. After serving as a soldier during World War I, Wilson married Lois Burnham in 1918 and became a successful Wall Street stockbroker. Traveling throughout the country, he evaluated companies for potential investors. Wilson lost all his money in the 1929 stock market crash, but continued for several years to earn a modest income by trading stocks. However, heavy drinking took a severe toll, and by 1933, Wilson was unemployed and living with Lois in her parents' Brooklyn home. He spent most of his days drinking gin while his wife worked at a local department store.

Wilson's alcohol dependency increased in severity, and he was hospitalized four times for alcohol-related conditions during 1933 and 1934. In November 1934, Wilson had visits from several acquaintances active with the Oxford Group; they encouraged him to follow its strategy for recovery. Wilson was intrigued, but continued to imbibe, and then in early December 1934, he went on an alcoholic binge that lasted for several days.

Fearful of undergoing delirium tremens without medical supervision, Wilson admitted himself on December 11 to Manhattan's Charles

B. Towns Hospital for Drug and Alcohol Addictions. Founded on Central Park West in 1901 by broker-businessman Charles Towns, it had long boasted a prestigious clientele and gained much success during the Roaring Twenties with the country's economic boom and concomitant rise in alcohol consumption. Under Dr. William Silkworth, the Towns' detoxification regimen included morphine, other psychoactive drugs, and belladonna—a substance that in large dosages can be hallucinogenic. After one of Wilson's friends visited and again urged him to adopt the Oxford Group's program for recovery, he was left alone in his hospital room.

Wilson fell into a state of despair, and then found himself pleading to God for help. In Wilson's memoir published some twenty years later and famous among AA members, he vividly recalled:

> All at once I found myself crying out, "If there is a God, let Him show Himself! I am ready to do anything, anything!" Suddenly the room lit up with a great white light. I was caught up into an ecstasy which there are no words to describe. It seemed to me, in the mind's eye, that I was on a mountain and that a wind not of air but of spirit was blowing. And then it burst upon me that I was a free man. Slowly the ecstasy subsided. I lay on the bed, but now for a time I was in a new world, a new world of consciousness. All about me and through me there was a wonderful feeling of Presence and I thought to myself, "So this is the God of the preachers!" A great peace stole over me and I thought, "No matter how wrong things seem to be, they are still all right. Things are all right with God and His world."[12]

As Maslow would say, Wilson had an intense nadir experience. Not surprisingly, he became frightened by it and reasoned that he had been hallucinating. He immediately recounted his experience to Dr. Silkworth, who, after a clinical interview, assured Wilson that he was not "going crazy" but rather affirmed that "there has been some basic psychological or spiritual event here. I've read about these things in the books. Sometimes spiritual experiences do release people from alcoholism."[13]

The next day, Wilson was presented with a copy of James's *The Varieties of Religious Experience* and "devoured [it] from cover to cover." Wilson never learned who had brought it to his hospital room, but assumed one of his Oxford Group friends had—a sensible deduction as

Varieties was on its recommended reading list. It is not difficult to guess what animated Wilson about *Varieties*, which described spiritual experiences and their transformative power. Wilson also read how spiritual experiences could come in many forms, ranging from sudden and profound epiphanies—as he had seemingly just experienced—to more gradual changes over time.

However, what affected Wilson most intensely was James's observation that "conversions" often come to people in dire situations—such as during external catastrophe or severe anguish. Though Wilson never said so explicitly, it seems likely that he found James's case study of Samuel Hadley especially inspiring, because it spoke so clearly to his own struggle and offered so much hope. Wilson would later remark:

> Spiritual experiences, James thought, could have objective reality; almost like gifts from the blue, they could transform people. Some were sudden brilliant illuminations; others came on very gradually. Some flowed out of religious channels; others did not. But nearly all had the great common denominators of pain, suffering, and calamity. Complete hopelessness and deflation at depth were almost required to make the recipient ready. The significance of all this burst upon me. *Deflation at depth*—yes, that was *it*. Exactly that had happened to me. [14]

Wilson continued:

> My thoughts began to race as I envisioned a chain reaction among alcoholics, one carrying this message and these principles to the next. More than I could ever want anything else, I now knew I wanted to work with other alcoholics. [15]

Such was the beginning of AA, originating in Wilson's nadir experience. In June 1935, the organization was officially founded in Akron, Ohio, with a second base of operations launched in New York City. In 1937, its third operational base was founded in Cleveland, Ohio, which became especially strong. By 1939, AA had broken its ties with the Oxford Group—a wise decision in views of the increasing unpopularity of its pro-Nazi leader Frank Buchman. During that same year, AA published *Alcoholics Anonymous*, which became known as the "Big Book." It described alcoholism as a lifetime disease and presented twelve steps to sobriety based on the self-surrender paradigm.

In early 1941, a favorable article about AA in the widely read *Saturday Evening Post* quickly catapulted national membership from two thousand to eight thousand and helped launch chapters in such major cities as Baltimore, Chicago, Detroit, Houston, Los Angeles, Philadelphia, and San Francisco. The first prison group was started at San Quentin in 1942, and two years later, the *A.A. Grapevine*, the organization's first newsletter, was published. Initially intended to communicate with U.S. armed forces members, the New York City–spawned newsletter soon went national, linking AA members and groups across the country.

By the early 1950s, AA had attracted more than ninety thousand people and had received awards from professional organizations such as the American Public Health Association. Mass media attention through positive portrayals in *Reader's Digest*, *Time Magazine*, and films like *Days of Wine and Roses* and *Come Back Little Sheba* elevated AA to unequalled dominance in popular understanding of alcohol recovery. Reflecting professional confidence in AA during that era, judges throughout the United States increasingly mandated legal offenders to AA and related twelve-step programs—all rooted in William James's seemingly solitary paradigm of addiction recovery.

In launching AA in the mid-1930s, Wilson clearly misinterpreted James's viewpoint in *Varieties* by declaring that self-surrender during despair is the *sole* model for alcoholism recovery. It is hardly surprising that Wilson, who had undergone a nadir experience similar to Hadley's as detailed by James, would seize upon this model and promote it vigorously to help countless others embroiled in the pain of alcohol addiction. Nevertheless, Wilson was significantly distorting James's pluralistic perspective on the nature of self-transformation. For not only did Wilson and his cohorts ignore James's recognition of conversion derived from joy and inspiration, but they also disregarded his vivid description in *Varieties* of alcohol usage as emanating from the basic human need for life affirmation and expanded consciousness.

By completely ignoring James's view that alcohol consumption comes from the legitimate need to experience self-transcendence, AA's founders were essentially demeaning the individual with alcohol dependency in a manner distant from James's own outlook. That is, they were removing a vital wellspring of emotional health in James's psychological system, and thus accentuating the qualities of pathology and powerlessness among people with alcohol dependency. Indeed, this stance has been central to AA since its inception—and it has unfortunately been carried over to the twelve-step programs as well. The consequences have been harmful and need to be redressed.

2

CHANGING OUR LANGUAGE, CHANGING OUR SUBJECTIVITY

The word "addiction" is both emotionally charged and culturally biased. By replacing addiction with "addictive behavior" and differentiating these behaviors from habits, we forge a new approach for this field, predicated upon viewing each person as a unique individual. In this way, people will determine across a far greater range of human behaviors exactly where they are. I am encouraging people to rethink what they think they know. I'm proposing an important shift in the conceptualization, definition, and treatment of what has been traditionally been called addiction—a word I make every effort to avoid using. First, though, let's define what I mean by these behaviors. For example, I'm often asked, "Is there such a thing as a *good* addiction?"

It's crucial to understand that *anything* can become addictive. Don't think in terms of just the consumption of alcohol or drugs. All habits, good or bad, and all addictive behaviors, good or bad, lie along a continuum. Therefore something (whether it's baking cookies, marathon running, or collecting nineteenth-century postcards) can be more or less habit-forming and more or less addictive in either a good or bad way. Notably, at the outset, both habits and addictive behavior are always learned. Later in this chapter, I'll provide a brief explanation about learning.

So, what differentiates an addictive behavior from a habit? Simply this: *the degree to which the costs of the behavior outweigh its benefits.* That's the key point to remember. Generally a habit will be at its worst only slightly more costly than its benefit; therefore, a habit lies within the mild range of becoming addictive. However, with an addictive behavior, the costs begin to far exceed its benefits. Typically, the individual gains no psychological well-being from actions, and has also lost command of autonomy. As a result, the individual is placed in the dangerous situation of potentially harming oneself or others.

For example, a good habit would be saying "thank you" frequently: expressing gratitude and appreciation as daily behavioral choices. In contrast, a bad habit would be to initiate arguments or belittling others, or insisting that one is always right in any discussion. If you were thinking I was going to describe a good habit as something hygienic like daily dental flossing, you're not really wrong. But remember that, more importantly in this context, how you present yourself to the world represents your subjective experience. It's doubtful that someone who is habitually ungrateful and unappreciative will enjoy positive relationships, regardless of daily hygiene. It's incongruent.

Of course, brushing your teeth daily is a good habit, as is refraining from biting your nails. You can also develop the good habit of drinking two glasses of red wine every day as recommended by the American Medical Association. Such behavior is generally believed by medical experts to lower your chances of developing diabetes or heart disease, or suffering a stroke. Or you can develop the excessive habit of drinking three or four glasses of wine daily. Why has drinking wine gone from good to not-so-good with a couple more glasses? Because once you start becoming intoxicated every day, you increase your risk for making poor choices. Such excessive behavior will also hinder your ability to gain restful sleep—a consequence that significantly affects both your familial and work responsibilities.

I make this distinction because in my coaching practice, I recently treated a thirty-five-year-old woman who was feeling lonely and depressed after a romantic breakup. Let's call her Ava. She began drinking a glass of wine every night to relax. Then one of Ava's friends told her that she probably had a drinking problem—from the friend's mistaken belief that moderate alcohol consumption, every night and alone indicates a disorder. Every behavior must be placed in context, which is why conventional checklist-screening is erroneously reductionist. If a person reports drinking alcohol daily, that behavior in itself isn't really a "sign" or "symptom" of anything.

An excessive habit can also involving constant swearing—that is, using obscenities. This repetitive action may offend some people and may conceivably lead to physical altercations and resulting harm—but by itself, it's just a bad learned behavior. But again remember: language is representative of one's subjective experience. An excessive good habit might be to read online news sites for two hours daily. Studying daily is a good habit. Reading, writing, and thinking are all wonderful activities. Only when these excessive behaviors take a person away from responsibilities and become problematic for effective functioning can these be viewed as serious problems.

Addictive behaviors can be beneficial, like physical exercise, love, sex, food, and listening to music. You probably know that the experience of being in love activates the same reward center of the brain and the chemical dopamine as do drugs. Yet these seemingly positive behaviors can be harmful if a preoccupation with them produces a dependency that interferes with other areas of one's life. Therefore, the major difference between a habit and something becoming more addictive is when the costs of the behavior far exceed its benefits.

For instance, Mark is a corporate accountant in his early thirties who lives alone. He enjoys one or two alcoholic beverages nightly to unwind with friends after work before commuting home. In my view, this can be considered a good habit. The benefits of friendship and conviviality outweigh the costs of consuming the alcoholic beverages.

However, suppose Mark begins to experience major stress at his job due to corporate downsizing and starts to drink so heavily that he calls in sick the next morning more and more often. Now the potential costs of Mark's drinking are far greater than the benefits. He has begun to be a potential danger to himself and others.

IS ROMANTIC LOVE ADDICTIVE?

All excessive habits and addictive behaviors can be conceptualized as "relationships" that people have learned to use to cope with life's challenges—and which limit their ability to negotiate effectively their perception of reality. It's therefore interesting to examine the role of romantic love in this context. In *Love and Addiction*, Stanton Peele in 1975 first suggested that romantic love is as addictive as any drug. He states, "We often say 'love' when we really mean, and are acting out, an addiction—a sterile, ingrown dependency relationship, with another person serving as the object of our need for security. This interpersonal dependency is not like an addiction, not something analogous to addiction; it is an addiction. It is every bit as much an addiction as drug dependency."[1] This idea was radical at a time when most professionals viewed addiction solely in terms of alcohol or drugs. Yet, I believe that Peele's key notion was that by identifying romantic love as addictive, he was also referring to the "relationships" that people form with certain types of behaviors. For example, Paul has a relationship with alcohol. Maxine has a relationship with food. And Robert has a relationship with heroin.

In the popular 1996 movie *Jerry Maguire* starring Tom Cruise, the now-famous romantic line, "You complete me," reinforced the naïve notion that a love partner not only makes your life better by enhancing your emotional well-being, but also erases your character flaws and defects. That's why in my view the search for a soul mate is often a distraction for dealing with psychological challenges and difficulties.

Why? Because addictive behavior always involves dependency, and a love relationship can certainly comprise with dependencies that fill emotional and psychological voids. Similar to substance-addictions involving drugs or alcohol—which are used to numb and mask our underlying problems in living—the habit of pursuing love relationships can produce the same euphoria and pleasure as substance-related dependencies. For as with any addictive behavior, the goal becomes seeking-out stimulation which is pleasurable and temporarily escaping from a perceived stressor or an emotionally triggering event.

In unhealthy love relationships, the dependency upon a romantic partner steadily increases. Cognitive and emotional pain are experienced when a partner is unavailable. In essence, one isn't as excited by a romantic partner as he/she was originally because a "tolerance" has been built up. Nevertheless, one has become increasingly dependent on having the emotional security of physical proximity. One becomes incapable of coping with extended periods of separation. It's no exaggeration to say that people in love relationships often suffer withdrawal symptoms when a breakup occurs. There are definite physical symptoms that are evident, such as sleeplessness, loss of appetite, headaches, and even heart palpitations. For the man or woman who is in "love with love," much of the reason for remaining with one's romantic ideal came from the fear and avoidance of the withdrawal experience.

But bear in mind: the most important relationship you'll ever have in your life is the one you have with yourself. American society places so such emphasis on the importance of being in a romantic partnership that people will often try denying or hiding their deficiencies to be valued by their partner. Yet until you learn more about yourself through self-discovery, you'll never choose the right love relationship to support both your own psychological well-being and that of your partner.

Addictive behaviors can be traced to many factors that originate in our early development. In this sense, addiction is better conceptualized as a learning and developmental disorder. A lack of resiliency in subjectively framing the experiences of our life due to unresolved early conflicts inhibits our ability to develop a mature, emotionally regulated personality. Our "self-talk" becomes needy, immature, and even obsessive. We idealize our romantic partners and internalize their apparent shortcomings. These types of psychological events are rooted in family of origin experiences.

THE ORIGINS OF ADDICTIVE BEHAVIORS

Although Sigmund Freud and Erik Erikson developed theories of human development that are now outdated in various respects, it's nonetheless true that psychological dysfunction can be traced to early childhood trauma, abuse, or neglect—and that children lacking in resiliency are more likely to become adults who are emotionally vulnerable and therefore susceptible to addictive relationships. This fact sheds light on why many people who manifest addictive behaviors as adults have shown such tendencies earlier in their lives. There's something to be said for the notion that a mother and father represent a child's first role models upon which all future relationships—from platonic friendships to passionate love—will be based.

How is this possible? Let's assume when you were between three and six years old, your father was seldom or never present in your life either because he divorced your mother, died, or simply was neglectful. Or that if he had been present, he was verbally or physically abusive toward you. Keep in mind that the brain is an organ of social adaptation;

therefore, these early experiences have affected your personality and your concomitant ideas about love relationships.

Some theorists suggest that a woman will search her entire life for a father-figure if her father wasn't emotionally available during her childhood. For example, she may repeatedly seek out older men with power and social status. She also may unconsciously attract into her life men who are emotionally distant in the same way as her father was while she was growing up.

Is all this just intriguing speculation? Not at all. For instance, one longitudinal study showed that children's personalities are fully developed by age seven and that many of their specific personality traits remained with them even forty years later.[2] This finding suggests that early childhood development not only forms the basis for our personality and susceptibility to mental and emotional challenges, but also contributes to the learned behaviors that comprise adult relationships.

According to Erikson, the first two life stages—encompassing basic trust versus mistrust, and autonomy versus shame or doubt—form the foundation for our lifelong sense of self-adequacy, self-worth, and ability to trust others. It's impossible to redo our childhood once we're grown up, giving therapists the difficult task of helping distressed adults acquire such emotional and social competencies in the absence of early familial learning.

ROMANTIC RELATIONSHIPS

From my coaching experience, it's undeniable that most relationships have elements of unconscious needs dating back to childhood. Indeed, some people use "relationships" to avoid dealing with adulthood. They're unconsciously seeking to be "parented" and are therefore attracted to their partners in an attempt to gain the attention, trust, and identity validation that was absent during their childhood development. Thus, you'll often hear an obese person jokingly referring to a "date" on Friday night with a quart of ice cream. There's a truth to this statement, for it *is* a relationship—providing comfort and familiarity. That bucket of ice cream temporarily reduces stress, anxiety, and depression, and temporarily fills the void of emptiness and loneliness.

Here's another general rule: the more intensely addictive the behavior, the bigger the underlying void. You can see this pattern with many people in their dating choices, for the partner is a reflection of that individuals' emotional state at that time in life. Love dependency is very real and is more prevalent in American society than is generally known.

In the children's book *The Missing Piece Meets the Big O*, Shel Silverstein presents this concept well. There is a "missing piece" which has been searching for a match, something to complete. After all, it's just a single piece and it needs to fit somewhere. It has met only with disappointment until it finds the Big O and now thinks this letter must be the special one. "I was hoping that perhaps I could roll with you," it says. However, the Big O wisely replies: "You cannot roll with me . . . but perhaps you can roll by yourself."[3] And so, the "missing piece" changes itself into something that can roll and it catches up with the Big O. Then they're able to roll together.

Humans have a self-determining nature and therefore they're going to do whatever they choose to do. In a thought experiment, let's take two scenarios of the "relationship" two people have with alcohol. Two people attend the same party. Each consumes several drinks. Each becomes intoxicated. One is happy and is celebrating a new romance, or a job promotion, or a personal best time running a 5K—and has an overall sense of happiness and life satisfaction. She expected to drink at the party and get intoxicated—and therefore chose not to drive herself home. Her relationship with alcohol was a positive experience.

The second person came in a bad mood to the party. She has just ended a romantic relationship or been experiencing stress and dissatisfaction at work—and overall lately is unhappy and depressed. She came to the party to escape these emotions and became rude and verbally aggressive while intoxicated. She chose to drive home and was stopped by a police car and cited for driving under the influence (DUI).

Two people, same party, same amount of alcohol, and each intoxicated. The only difference was in their underlying state of mind: that is, how they experienced themselves. Their subjectivity differed greatly. These were the preconditions that lead to their subsequent behaviors and the choices they made.

As we know, the language within the "addiction industry" is standardized. Its focus is on pathology, medicalization, and pharmaceutical treatments. Its language is deficit-based, with words like "powerless" and "disease." As another thought experiment, let's take two narratives of the same twenty-four-year old, Mexican-American female, Carla, who has been arrested for a DUI and for possessing a small amount of marijuana. She also had in her possession an assortment of prescription painkillers.

Carla has been depressed in attempting to clarify her sexual identity issues. She found herself getting high and engaging in self-destructive sexual relationships with men to prove to herself that she was desirable to them and not really attracted to women. Sometimes when Carla was intoxicated, she'd kiss another woman. She lives at home with her two older sisters and a younger brother. Carla's father abandoned the family when she was four years old, and both her father and stepfather had physically abused her. Carla's mother was always anxious, had low self-esteem, and allowed Carla's father to control the relationship.

In scenario one, Carla goes through the conventional treatment protocol. She may be assigned to a drug counselor, mandated to attend drug and alcohol educational classes, and perhaps mandated to attend AA meetings. In each of these instances, she will probably be told in one way or another that she is an "alcoholic" and a "drug addict," is "powerless" and "in denial," and has a "disease" like cancer or diabetes. Most likely, too, Carla's drug counselor is having difficulty from his own substance use and in trying to remain abstinent. Yet, they are still disseminating information about alcohol and drug usage to an essentially unfamiliar person.

Carla is accustomed to being victimized for most of her life. She is vulnerable and susceptible to persuasion, having no other basis by which to frame her subjectivity. Carla views the world as an unsafe place with no security. She struggles for control, but is told that she is powerless over her drinking and drugging. Carla's creative control over her thinking is subdued as she is reprimanded for not submitting to those demanding her conformity. Such an approach reinforces Carla's sense of being a victim, her sexual-identity crisis, her low self-esteem, and overall feelings of dread.

However, in scenario two, Carla appears before a healthy-minded counselor. This person is client-centered and not myopic or dogmatic—not a reductionist who finds the term "disease" to be useful in treatment. Rather than seeking quick answers involving screening tools or pontificating useless knowledge, this counselor provides compassion and empathy. The primary focus is on how Carla experiences herself; her sexual identity and early abuse are important underlying problems to be effectively addressed. Because Carla lives in a neighborhood in which substance abuse is prevalent, it doesn't indicate that she has a predetermined, genetically influenced disorder, rather it's her environment that contributes to making her more vulnerable.

Carla's counselor can say, "This is a golden opportunity now for you to grow and change, to get unstuck and live your life to its fullest potential. You're not powerless." With her counselor's help, Carla can find her voice. She can creatively control her subjectivity by broadening the framework of her thinking. Carla isn't "diseased." She learned certain maladaptive behaviors to cope—and she can certainly learn new, positive behaviors as well.

Excessive habits and addictive behaviors are *learned.* They represent choices that people make to cope with their inability to direct effectively their subjective perception of reality. For such people, the best outcome is to gain help in unlearning these behaviors. This necessitates insight into how they learned these ineffectual actions and also learning how to replace these with better choices. By doing so, they are "rewiring" their brain. Interpersonal biology teaches that because the brain is an organ of social adaptation, we can overcome the effects of early childhood events through *neuroplasticity.* This term refers to our brain's ability to change its internal structuring by the creation of new neurons and the many connections that they form.

This process is enhanced by enriched environments in which learning is best assimilated. At the core of hardwired subjectivity is a person's perception of fear and an ability to cope with stress, for these inhibit new learning. Therefore, as long as fear and stress are the chief factors shaping a person's daily subjective experience, the brain's adaptive power will be hampered. Conventional treatment approaches through applying such labels as "disease," "powerlessness," "abstinence only," "chronic," "lifelong," "in denial," "relapse," and "recovery" are ineffectual. Why? Because these only serve to inhibit the hippocampus and prefrontal cortex areas of the brain—and keep activated the amygdala (the brain's fear center). This process not only keeps fear and stress continuously active, but creates the preconditions for unconscious, automatically stored responses to be triggered again and again.

ADDICTIVE BEHAVIORS AND LEARNING

If you ever took Introductory Psychology, you've been exposed at least briefly to a section on learning. Do you remember studying about the scientist who rang a bell and made his dogs salivate at the sound? His name was Ivan Pavlov and he was a Russian physiologist in the early 1900s. While investigating the digestive system of dogs, he discovered what is known as "classical conditioning." Do you recall the psychologist who watched children mimic their parents' behavior and then aggressively struck a Bobo clown doll? His name was Albert Bandura and he developed the concept of "observational learning." How about the psychologist who tried classical conditioning methods on a little boy named Albert? That man was John B. Watson and he launched the field of behaviorism in the United States soon after Pavlov's seminal work.

How about the psychologist who placed his own young daughter in a box-like device that either rewarded or withdrew rewards for a specific action she committed? He was B. F. Skinner and he originated such concepts as operant conditioning—encompassing positive reinforcement, negative reinforcement, and punishment. Most college students exposed to such fundamental material in introductory psychology don't necessarily understand how these experiments relate to their own learning process in everyday life. But these experiments certainly do.

By way of analogy, I like to use the model of addictive behavior as a means to explain these concepts to my students. Certainly the brain is very complex, and in no way do I seek to minimize this fact. But I will attempt to use simple ideas so that you can better understand how addictive behaviors are always learned.

First, let's assume that your brain resembles a super computer. This is your operating system. That's your *nature*. All your particular life experiences, beginning with those in the womb, comprise your software. That's *nurture*. Some of these experiences are wonderful, even ecstatic—what psychologist Abraham Maslow called "peak experiences." Some aren't so pleasant. Generally, we remember the positive experiences and store away the unpleasant ones.

Second, mentally we always function simultaneously on both a conscious and unconscious level. This is what's known as our dual-track mind. That is, part of our mind operates consciously and involves effort, and the other part operates unconsciously and automatically. Thus, we can listen enjoyably to music and think happily about our upcoming vacation while driving our car safely through dense city traffic.

Learning is a process that produces relatively enduring change in behavior or knowledge as a result of experience. Classical conditioning is a learning process that involves the repeated pairing of a neutral stimulus with a response-producing stimulus, until the neutral stimulus elicits the same response. How so? Because the organism now associates the neutral stimulus with the response-producing stimulus.

For example, Jason is a young stockbroker who repeatedly *pairs* the neutral stimulus of a $1 bill with the unconditioned stimulus of a line of cocaine. After spending a month in rehab, Jason leaves feeling worried and emotionally vulnerable. Sitting alone in a café the next day, he pulls a $1 bill from his pocket. Instantly, Jason's mind *associates* the bill with the pleasure of cocaine—and he suddenly begins to crave it. Within an hour, Jason has returned to cocaine usage. Remember, one of the reasons why people often overdose right after leaving rehab is that they haven't learned anything new in order to cope with their troubling subjective experiences. And, they no longer have the same tolerance they had when they were using regularly. They start using again like they used to. The result is often disastrous and even fatal.

Operant conditioning is the basic learning process that involves changing the probability that a response will be repeated by manipulating the consequences of the response.

Within this learning paradigm, positive reinforcement is anything that strengthens a particular behavior, such as "getting high" on a drug. That is, positive reinforcement encourages the behavior to continue.

Negative reinforcement is anything that eliminates or weakens a particular behavior—for example, drinking alcohol to reduce stress and anxiety. The desire not to feel stress and anxiety makes the act of continuing to drink more likely. I propose to abandon the term negative reinforcement as first established by B. F. Skinner. It's quite confusing, as many students erroneously associate negative reinforcement with punishment. In my view, this term is needlessly complicated; the usage simply of the word "reinforcement" is sufficient.

Rather than referring to positive and negative reinforcement, it's more helpful to understand that reinforcement provides two main functions. That is, a learned behavior is likely to continue when it (1) provides a perception of pleasure, and (2) when it removes or lessens pain or discomfort, such as stress, depression, or anxiety. Once learned, these experiences become unconscious stored responses and automatic. These are triggered when the individual experiences something they perceive to be challenging, threatening or harmful and attempts to cope with these events through a particular behavior.

Think of a DUI arrest as a form of punishment. In the United States, tens of thousands of people are currently incarcerated for nonviolent drug offenses. They are being punished for their behavior. However, rather than learning new skills and appropriate behaviors that will help them upon release from prison, many learn how to become even more criminally minded. This is one explanation for the high percentage of recidivism. In my view, incarceration for such offenses maintains the problem—and fails to act as a deterrent. It certainly doesn't teach offenders how to change their drug dependency—and may even reinforce such behavior because the environment reinforces the need to conform to survive, thus maintaining the problem. As Nelson Mandela declared, "It is said that no one truly knows a nation until one has been inside its jails. A nation should not be judged by how it treats its highest citizens, but its lowest ones."[4]

Now, let's put this all together. Jessica is a forty-five-year-old divorced mother with two grown children. She is employed as a clerical supervisor at a large city agency in the Midwest. Jessica has always had low self-esteem, and is unhappy about both her personal and professional life. Jessica learned that she gained a temporary "high" from using cocaine. It was pleasurable—*reinforcing*, so she learned to do it over and over again. Jessica also learned that she temporarily lessened her emotional pain and distress by getting high—and this consequence was also *reinforcing*.

The important thing to understand is that these behaviors are operating on both a conscious and unconscious level. That's why they are so difficult to stop. The brain has been wired. It now needs to be unwired and rewired by reducing fear and stress, and by enhancing the brain's adaptive powers. Mainstream rehabs cannot have long-term benefits, for abstinence alone does not change these learning processes. Without new learning and a better quality of thinking, the individual subjective experience is dampened.

3

THE REALITY OF HUMAN EXPERIENCE

We all experience pain. To be human is to suffer at times. Eminent spiritual teachers throughout history remind us that pain and suffering are an inescapable part of life. Excessive habits and addictive behaviors are the ways you cope with problems in everyday living, but can be replaced with new ways of coping by challenging your debilitating thoughts and beliefs. Practical solutions to these problems are available if you look in the right place. That's within. People are the stories they tell themselves about themselves. Your daily personal narration gives your life direction, meaning, and purpose.

In my coaching approach, I see every person as a unique individual, having shaped and formed a personality through specific life experiences. We bring diverse and subjective experiences to our various relationships and cope with our individualized or culturally influenced pain through learned behaviors. For this reason, I feel that it's essential to support, respect, and value all people with the specific intention of contributing toward their ability to achieve joy and life satisfaction as they define it.

In this book, I've been mindful to be inclusive. Today, many approaches to dealing with excessive habits and addictive behaviors are structured to find quick fixes, assign labels, and formulate generalizations. One of the unfortunate results of this trend is that we lose the dynamics created by embracing differences. Any form of coaching, teaching, or disseminating knowledge should seek to embrace diversity. This process necessitates not merely recognizing differences among groups of people on this planet, but appreciating and respecting such differences. This worldview encompasses individuals and groups of different religions, ethnicities, ages, disabilities, sexual orientations, educational levels, political affiliations, and socioeconomic status. We are all part of humanity and the human condition.

Nobody can change someone else's self-determining nature. No amount of therapy. No amount of drugs. No amount of group support. People change when they want to, or they don't change. As an educator, I challenge my students to be critical thinkers and to take personal responsibility for their learning. I review concepts repeatedly and encourage them to think outside the box. As a critical thinker, you should always ask yourself: Does this make sense? Is it logical? How can I use this information to make changes in my life?

For the most part, people become preoccupied with substances and destructive behavior patterns in an attempt to mask or hide from their emotional pain. It's usually related to unresolved early learning experiences, past or present trauma, anxiety, stress, and depression. These are the problems that most people with addictive behaviors are facing— regardless of their age, economic status, gender, race, religion, educational level, ethnicity, or socioeconomic status. *The substance or behavior isn't really the problem.* Rather, it's usually the result of your misguided attempt to find a solution to your troubles by avoiding them. Your life problems are contributing to your addictive behavior, not the other way around. It doesn't matter what the behavior is: whether it involves alcohol, illegal drugs, pain medication, sex, shopping, gambling, smoking, eating, or Internet use. If you engage in the behavior to escape from emotional pain, then you need to better understand why you're doing so.

Because of our needs for control and certainty, particular behaviors that are used for coping begin to control you—something you feel you can't be happy without, and eventually, something you're positive you can't live without. At their core, excessive habits and addictive behaviors are essentially actions you take, specific things you do, to relieve pressure or discomfort of some kind. People who are preoccupied with alcohol will feel compelled to drink when life's problems begin to rise up and stare them in the face. One who is addicted to drugs will do whatever is necessary to get another "quick fix" when beginning to feel uneasy. For example, a young woman preoccupied by food will turn to overeating for both comfort and relaxation when she becomes physically stressed, emotionally upset, or emotionally drained.

The particular substance which you're challenged by helps relieve your pain for a brief duration, but then always requires more. Why? Because you build up a tolerance, which, in turn, sets you up for the eventual downward spiral in your life experienced at some point by virtually all who suffer from these types of behaviors. You'll find that you typically follow a specific sequence of events—starting from when the unwanted feelings first arise, to obtaining and ingesting that substance or engaging in the behavior, to the relief that comes, to the letdown and remorse phase—to the time that elapses before this cycle starts all over again.

Understanding this concept clearly as it applies to your unique acting-out patterns is the foundation of how you'll learn to *deconstruct* each feeling and corresponding action. You personally orchestrated these actions. You can now undo them. You must unravel your specific behavioral sequence to truly understand it. You'll then be able to initiate new, positive actions to finally break free from the control that addictive behaviors exert over your life. My guidance is designed to help people understand their addictive behavior as a *learned coping response* which is now part of their inner world.

Addictive behaviors are human experiences. They lie along a continuum in terms of severity. As people become more familiar with themselves their first goal will be to determine where they are on this spectrum. One end involves healthy functioning, and the other end involves being severely distressed. The determination is where the person is at the moment. Is the behavior rather normal and a fairly rare occurrence, something mild, or moderate in severity? Or is this more serious? Are these behaviors relatively newly formed or chronic? Certainly, you may have a common, relatively harmless behavior like frequent jogging, reading, watching TV, texting, or drinking an alcoholic beverage after work. Such behaviors are reinforcing, because they bring you pleasure, and so you engage in them daily. Is your behavior fairly normal in most areas of your life—but because you're distressed about a particular unresolved problem, do you wonder if your occasional three beers after work means you have a drinking problem? Remember, the issue is never black or white, good or bad, all or nothing.

Think about it logically. Should someone who drank a pint of Jack Daniels almost daily for twenty years—a behavior which has resulted in liver damage—be diagnosed the same way as a fourteen-year-old adolescent who is physically abused at home and subsequently begins drinking beer with other troubled youths to numb the emotional pain? Treatment needs to be kinder.

Clinicians need to be more compassionate. It's better to be curious than need to be right.

Your internal dialogue and language must be empowering, not negative or deficit-based. Look to be self-determined and more autonomous in your thinking. The helping process should encourage more compassion and empathy and seek to empower people not reinforce a generalized deficit-based language.

Drinking too much, recreational and prescription drug abuse, excessive overeating, and obsessively acting out with sex or pornography—as well as other unwanted addictive behaviors—are ways of dealing with life's stresses for people who are fearful, lack positive coping skills, or have low self-esteem and meager self-confidence. When you aren't doing what you want in life, you choose certain behaviors as a way to soothe yourself. For not being able to define who you are as an individual and achieve meaningful goals can be agonizing. Finding your own identity separate from other people and painful past experiences can be difficult to achieve. But it's not impossible. You have to find your power and gain your own authentic voice. This cannot occur if others use labels to explain away your unhappiness and lack of fulfillment no matter how rich or poor, successful or challenged you may be.

Start by asking yourself some basic questions: Who am I? What do I want my life to be about? How can I contribute to humanity? What are the stories you tell yourself about yourself? How do you frame your reality? Are you basically an optimistic person or pessimistic? Do you see the glass half full or half empty? Do you take personal responsibility for mistakes and give credit to others? Do you take the credit and blame others? How you creatively construct your own subjectivity is how you will experience and respond to life challenges. Think about the primary relationships in your life: those involving your parents and siblings, spouse and children, coworkers and boss, friends and neighbors. Is there ample growth in these relationships, or have some become dysfunctional or empty? Is your marriage joyful with peak experiences, or are you constantly being triggered negatively by your spouse in an increasingly stagnant relationship? Do you feel that life is an endless battle of self-preservation filled with rivalry, antagonism, chaos, and drama? This thinking, feeling, and believing will affect your relationships.

If you had a difficult childhood and find yourself spending most of your time in dysfunctional relationships or an unfulfilling career, or being manipulated and triggered unconsciously all day long by our "more is better" consumerist culture, is it any wonder that you're preoccupied with certain behaviors? You may well be second-guessing yourself constantly and feeling frustrated and insecure—a situation that leads to vacillating back and forth about which action to take to find true contentment.

Does your inner dialogue sound something like this? "I'm unhappy." "I'm afraid." "It's not fair." "I feel so alone." If you're drinking too much alcohol, or smoking too much pot, or overeating, or taking too many pain pills, on a deeper level it's not really about any of that—for all these behaviors are simply *red flags* telling you there are problems to address. For example, the problem of being unhappy is being at odds with your desired self, and instead suffering in quiet desperation, knowing you could be so much more. But self-defeating thinking maintains the problems. You can't seek excuses or let fear stop you, because fear evokes anxiety, anxiety evokes confusion, and confusion evokes all kinds of daily self-created trials and tribulations that throw you completely off course. You need to be empowered and embolden yourself. You need courage. Your addictive behavior is not your main problem. It's not like a headache. You don't take a pill and the behavior goes away. You can't simply change your subjective experiences or how you genuinely feel about yourself when you look into the mirror unless you change the quality of your thinking.

Your negative thoughts and feelings and your lack of effective coping skills are reinforced by those whose intentions may be good but who have the need to dismiss complex human experiences with outdated labels and absolute certainties, or what I refer to as *old-school thinking*. Gaining self-control requires your need to rethink, reprocess, and integrate new ways of responding to environmental stressors. A lot of your nervous system's conditioned response behavior goes back to your childhood, such as involving poor role modeling from parents, abuse, or neglect and the subsequent lack of resiliency. Don't believe the dominant view that you have a disease, and that if you merely abstain from alcohol, drugs, unhealthy foods, or pain medication, then you'll be fine. Such a view is incredibly shortsighted and unrealistic. Its convenience has led us away from embracing our roles as part of humanity and appreciating human experiences as human without fearing them.

In the brain, dopamine functions as a neurotransmitter—that is, a chemical released by nerve cells to send signals to other nerve cells. Dopamine plays a major role in reward-motivated behavior. All drugs of abuse affect dopamine directly or indirectly. But keep in mind, dopamine is also necessary for learning and memory. The presence of dopamine, the sensitivity to it, or the lack thereof—which is part of the popular theoretical basis for the disease model of addiction—is simply our need as humans to seek stimulation.

People with addictive behaviors are stimulation-seekers. Certainly, drugs and alcohol are two ways to gain stimulation. Extreme sports like skydiving or hot air ballooning offer additional ways. People choose what they like by what they've learned that allows them to have fun, relax, and escape from daily stresses. Many means exist to obtain stimulation. If some people tend to do so in more dangerous ways than others because of a desire for a dopamine rush—does that mean one may have a disease, but the other doesn't? Each person is a unique individual with a specific set of life circumstances. If you are a clinician making an assessment, measuring someone's subjective well-being is more important than simply looking at a checklist of symptom choices.

Undeniably, AA and other twelve-step programs have helped many people deal with their addictive behaviors effectively if for no other reason than the sheer numbers of people exposed to these approaches and the convenience of their availability. If you're getting the help you need from attending these meetings, then certainly keep doing so. However, AA and twelve-step programs don't work for everyone. Indeed, they may be extremely constricting for some people because the twelve-step treatment approach is old-school thinking, outdated, and narrow-minded. Unfortunately, many people have a tendency to settle for partial solutions or accept the false comforts of whatever group-based approach to which they're exposed. Some patients are comfortable in the middle of a herd—even if the herd is wandering close to a cliff.

In many ways, AA's twelve-step programs are burdened by their original tenets and the various fundamentalist interpretations of its treatment approach by overzealous members who may indeed contribute any long-term abstinence to attending meetings. This situation can cause new attendees to be unfairly subjected to social pressure, misinformation, and shame messages regarding addictive behaviors. This is why many may go to AA, but most do not stick around. Furthermore, an analysis of the most comprehensive studies on AA suggest "that roughly 5 to 8 percent of the total population of people who enter AA are able to achieve and maintain sobriety for longer than one year."[1]

Statistics reveal that the majority of people diagnosed with addictive behavior disorders are functioning and productive in many areas of their life. You must become an expert concerning your own habits of self-deception. Most of us deceive ourselves with little dramas all the time. We have blind spots of which we're not even aware. We intentionally avoid seeing things because we believe that what we'll uncover about ourselves will be too painful to bear. Self-deception is so insidious because its very process "covers its tracks"—so when you look back, you not only don't know what you deceived yourself about, but you also don't see the method by which you did so. In *Vital Lies, Simple Truths: The Psychology of Self-Deception*, Daniel Goleman summarizes the matter perfectly in stating, "Self-deception, by its very nature, is the most elusive of mental facts. Self-deception operates both at the level of the individual mind, and in our collective awareness of the group. To belong to a group of any sort, sometimes the tacit price of membership is to agree not to question anything that challenges the group's way of doing things."[2]

Many people face this dilemma when they begin attending AA's twelve-step meetings and disagree with the ideas of powerlessness, the disease model of addictive behaviors, and the need for lifelong recovery that are stressed at these gatherings. Some men and women stay because they don't know any other options. To AA's credit, you can find a meeting on seemingly every block in every city on any day, anywhere in the United States. Yet, people quit addictive behaviors on their own all the time. For example, nicotine is an addictive drug that some experts say is harder to quit than heroin.[3]

In the late 1980s, when the dangers of smoking became widely known, about half of all Americans who smoked addictively quit. Remarkably, according to a May 1990 report in the *Journal of the American Medical Association*, nearly 90 percent of them did so without any treatment at all.[4] Today that figure would probably be around 50–60 percent because of numerous cessation approaches like nicotine gums, patches, prescription medication, and hypnosis. Ironically, AA has a Nicotine Anonymous group, which seems counterintuitive since smoking is quite popular among those abstaining from alcohol. Did the person you know who permanently stopped smoking attend a treatment center or twelve-step meetings? I would guess not. Would 90 percent, or 50 percent, or any percent of people diagnosed with cancer go into remission on their own without treatment? So much then for the addictive substance of nicotine being comparable to an actual disease like cancer. An example of the misleading use of language.

This situation is more common than you might think. For example, a 1993 research paper, "Vietnam Veterans' Rapid Recovery from Heroin Addiction: A Fluke or Normal Expectations?" studied heroin use by American soldiers during the Vietnam War and revealed some startling discoveries about addiction recovery with and without the benefit of treatment. Researchers found that in 1970–1971, 45 percent of all American soldiers in Vietnam tried narcotics of which 20 percent claimed to have been addicted. In the first year of their return back to the United States, only 5 percent of those who were addicted in Vietnam remained so. Further, only 12 percent of them continued to be addicted at any time in the first three years after their return home to the United States. They also found that the "relapse" rate was higher for veterans who received treatment for their addiction than it was for those men who received no treatment at all. The researchers concluded that, "One of the original motivations for the study was the Veteran's Administration's concern that returning addicts would overtax their services; but the anticipated large demand never occurred."[5]

This is an often cited study because during the 1970s heroin was thought to be a drug that once a person was hooked on it, they never would be able to free themselves. To me this addictive behavior shows the learned associations made by soldiers away from home and living with chronic levels of daily stress and fear. The subjective experience of killing another human being and watching others around you be killed would be traumatic.

Think about it logically. Could the explanation for these findings simply be that the trauma and horror of war created so much fear and stress in American soldiers that, to numb their pain, drug use became a common occurrence to cope? In addition, by changing their environment, could it be that after returning home and being reunited with loving family and friends, taking drugs was no longer necessary? I think it does. In a similar way, we have taken our eye off the ball in focusing attention, time, and resources to the "war on drugs," when the real war is at home with the overdiagnosing, and overprescribing of prescription drugs. Add to this the reality that doctors and politicians receive financial support from the pharmaceutical industry, and drug problems in this country will not change no matter how many brain-imaging studies are conducted. Today, heroin use is on the rise as a consequence of the prescription painkiller epidemic. We have been socially indoctrinated by the media to respond to this type of emotionally charged news with fear.

What this scientific study on heroin use in Vietnam and numerous others like it reveals is that too much drinking, drug use, overeating, sex, gambling, and all other addictive behaviors are only just that— behaviors. Learned behaviors. We live in a culture in which the medical-psychiatric establishments diagnose and label nearly every undesirable behavior in people. A pill or medical intervention is then prescribed in an often futile attempt to "cure." To achieve this end, such behaviors that affect nearly all of us to varying degrees are reduced to biology and then redefined as diseases. More often than not, the medical establishment promotes the disease model to patients regarding both substance use and addictive behaviors to ensure ongoing sales of pharmaceutical drugs and such symptom-management approaches as in-patient treatment facilities. Real solutions are bad for profits as they remove the patient from the endless revenue stream.

Many people use alcohol or drugs recreationally on a regular basis to relax and celebrate their lives. They're individuals from all walks of life who have careers, run companies, and are highly productive. Imbibing wine or smoking marijuana are behaviors. It's the reason *why* you're engaging in them that's crucial. If you're having a glass of wine with your spouse because you want to celebrate your love together, that's one thing. But if you're drinking alcohol a lot because you're highly stressed about a job you detest and bills are piling up, or you're unhappy in your romantic relationship—these are the problems to address. You may feel like you're helpless, you may feel like you lack options— but that's because you have no references or resources, and so you are limited in a quest for help-seeking. We put ourselves in positions mentally where we can't see a way out, where we don't see any other choice but to give in to conventionality. The future is in the moment. You can rewrite your life story moment to moment. Each day you can be mindful. Each day you can address the quality of your thinking. What would make you really happy and excited about your life so that you'd never consider sabotaging your success with addictive behaviors? In this way you are actually self-assessing and challenging your own thought and belief system. By improving the quality of your thinking you will improve the quality of the language you use to represent yourself in the world. The quality of your language will then be apparent in the authenticity observed in your behavior.

A single-minded approach to treating addictive behaviors isn't feasible because people's relationships are always individualistic. The reality is that the United States has experienced very little change in the yearly percentage of people who are estimated to meet the criteria for an alcohol or drug problem. As of 2013, more than 22.7 million people met this criterion. Every year, only about 13 percent of these individuals actually seek treatment.[6] Millions more do not meet the criteria for having a problem but may desire some counseling to better understand their behavior, perhaps concerned by an increased use of a substance. Where should they go? Who could they talk to that would listen to their stories and properly assess their life challenges without lumping them in with everyone else? Many people overcome addictive behavior on their own without any treatment. The primary way they accomplish this is by uncovering the underlying problems that compel them to self-medicate and self-soothe in the first place and then choosing a course of action that is most appropriate for them to resolve it. Seen behaviorally, addictive behaviors are an effect—a result of attempting to deny, hide, or have no awareness that these behaviors have been learned and have now become unconscious automatic responses. Stanford University's eminent psychologist Albert Bandura declared in a major research study that, "Alcohol abuse is not a monolithic condition with an inevitable progression but rather, a multi-determined pattern varying from person to person in its severity and causation."[7] Everyone is different. Everyone has their own unique subjective experiences.

Research psychologist Bruce K. Alexander cautions that, "The world faces a deadly serious problem of addiction to drugs and countless other habits and pursuits. Bringing this problem under control will require a better conceptualization of addiction than the one that is currently being globally circulated by official sources."[8]

His Dislocation Theory draws attention to social causes of addiction that can be remedied only through major changes in the status quo. Knowing that the "Official View of Addiction" doesn't threaten the status quo in any serious way helps to explain how it has become so deeply entrenched in the public mind and in officialdom, despite its conceptual weakness and practical ineffectiveness.

Alexander argues that the reason that America's corporations and mass media define addiction almost exclusively as a disease marked by an involvement with drugs or alcohol that is harmful to individuals or society as a whole is because they want to avoid focusing on government and corporate addictions to warfare and consumerism. Such a focus would jeopardize their profits and control. Alexander suggests that a better definition of addiction would be: "The overwhelming involvement with any pursuit whatsoever that is harmful to individuals and/or society."[9]

What does this mean for you? That the prevailing wisdom in our culture regarding addictive behaviors and the solutions offered to address them by governmental, private, and religious institutions may not be the best approach for people today in the twenty-first century. We're all unique in our stories and the circumstances by which we choose to act in self-destructive ways.

When we allow the social impress to influence our perception of reality we lose our power, our voice, and our autonomy. Thus we are subjugated and become disconnected from humanity.

4

LOVE, APPROVAL, AND VALIDATION

We all want to love and to be loved. Through others our lives are given direction, meaning, and purpose. The desire for love, approval, and validation can be life-affirming and healthy when there's balance in your life. But if you have an outsized need for constant recognition from others, it can become a problem leading to addictive behaviors. We develop our need for love and approval during early childhood attachment. The brain is a social organ that is wiring itself during this developmental time. Childhood experiences involving primary caregivers that were perceived to be lacking in love and approval unconsciously create the need and motivation to find it through-out life. This dynamic is prevalent in AA's twelve-step meetings, where new attendees often form unconscious family-of-origin connections with other troubled members. This situation fosters a psychological dependence on group participation and comes from an unconscious attraction to comfort and familiarity.

To receive love, approval, and validation many people will tolerate inappropriate behavior in others just to feel connected in a social, work, or romantic situation. Because such people are deficient in their ability to set boundaries, develop adequate self-esteem, have lower self-worth, and have learned to behave in emotionally unstable ways, their relationships are filled with needless anxiety and drama—and consequently, they rarely secure the healthy love and approval they seek. This situation creates a void that is filled with addictive behaviors which then act like *relationships* which are used to fulfill emotional needs and to cope.

Sharon is a twenty-four-year-old marketing assistant for a social media company. She is a people-pleaser and constantly seeks reassurance that she's doing a good job. However, in Sharon's efforts to be competent, she frequently makes mistakes and is criticized by her boss, whose approval she desperately seeks. This situation often causes Sharon to exhibit passive-aggressive behaviors like making intentional mistakes just to get her boss's attention. Her boss reprimands her and because Sharon is so sensitive, she takes the criticisms personally. She becomes depressed because in her self-appraisal, she can't do anything right. Because Sharon has an intense need for love and approval, she continues to behave in negative ways to get attention, even though her behavior could cause her to be fired. It's counterintuitive but she has learned this way of presenting herself to others.

Doug is a forty-four-year-old insurance agent who's very needy emotionally. At a recent family gathering, he told a lot of jokes and talked to almost everyone. From the outside looking in, you'd think Doug has a wonderful personality and is quite amiable, but a cousin commented that she thought Doug's jokes were inappropriate and his storytelling overbearing. Doug was extremely hurt by this remark and became obsessed with getting his cousin to "forgive" him. When Doug contacted her and she didn't return his call, he immediately began obsessing over what he'd said or what he might have done to offend her. Doug's need for approval from almost everyone he encounters is so strong that he often becomes anxious and insecure after a minor misunderstanding.

A lot of the emotional pain that people experience comes from an unhealthy need for love, approval, and validation from others. Despite their outward appearance of happiness and competence, many people experience existential anxiety, fear, and insecurity. Despite their high social or economic standing, many people feel they need the approval of others to be happy. Think about your life today. How often do you experience joy, happiness, and life satisfaction? How often are you mindful and present in your thoughts and actions? You'll find that many of the preconditions that lead to addictive behaviors—particularly feelings of chronic stress, anxiety, depression, low self-esteem, low self-worth, anger, and emptiness—are directly related to your need for love, approval, and validation. Each one of these words conjures a void for many people—and until you're able to address your underlying problems and values, by becoming receptive for the need to expand the quality of your thinking and your subjective experiences, you will remain stuck, discontent, and forlorn.

In my experience, I've found that the preoccupation with seeking love, approval, and validation is far more prevalent than any substance-related problems—and that it's an underlying contributing cause in most addictive behaviors. We live in an attention-seeking society. The quest for love, approval, and validation from others is healthy to a certain degree because it forms the basis for long-term relationships with significant others, family, and friends. But it becomes unhealthy when the pursuit becomes obsessive. Since the foundation of healthy self-worth is being true to oneself and displaying integrity and courage, if you lack these traits you'll always seek out others for reassurance. What does it mean to be "addicted" to love? Some common signs include constantly seeking attention and recognition, experiencing frequent negative self-talk or an ambivalent personal narrative, taking on the responsibilities of others, saying "yes" when you really want to say "no," and feeling as though no matter how well you do, it's never sufficient.

Do you feel that your happiness and well-being are dependent upon gaining love, approval, and validation from others? Do you feel that you're not good enough? Do you find it difficult to handle the pain of disapproval or rejection from others? Being preoccupied with these things is a hard way to live. Your relationships begin with idealization and hope but dissipate into the reality of disappointment and devaluing. Your thoughts and feelings are like a pendulum—swinging back and forth from feeling wonderful when you get your perceived love or to feeling frustration and despair when your source of love ignores you, gets angry, or leaves. An unhealthy need for love, approval, and validation can usually be traced to early childhood development where personality is shaped and formed by the perception of learning experiences, abuse, trauma, abandonment, or poor role-modeling.

Lisa Firestone states that our "critical inner voice" we have learned to use—thinking that it protects us from being abandoned or hurt—actually maintains the feelings of guilt and shame. This manifests itself in sabotaging intimate relationships and is seen in self-destructive behaviors.[1]

Three things are occurring early in life: (1) The brain is developing. (2) The personality is being shaped and formed. (3) The foundation for future mental distress is being wired. If you were abused or neglected as a child, you may still have pain, sadness, and false beliefs about yourself and the world that are now stored unconsciously. You may still be longing for the warmth and safety you never received all those years ago. When you're preoccupied with getting your needs met after your personality has been formed around seven years old, you're constantly in a state of regression or arrested development. Instead of learning to be self-compassionate and learning to be more mindful to externalize the self-criticisms and to rethink them objectively, you "hand over" your unmet childhood needs to others—making those people responsible for your feelings. Such expectations always cause the intense pain of low self-esteem and leads you to be dependent upon others for your sense of value. As long as you make other people responsible for providing your self-worth, you'll never find the love, peace, and joy that you seek. You also learn to be dependent on things outside of yourself. This will also inhibit your self-confidence which provides for growth and change.

Jessica is a thirty-three-year-old woman whose father left the family when she was in kindergarten. For many years, she's been attracting emotionally distant men. In Jessica's last romantic relationship, her partner was so hurtful emotionally that it caused her to become depressed. This situation triggered an episode of binge eating as a way to deal with the depression—basically caused by her need for love from men in an effort to fill the void left by her father's absence. As an adult, Jessica still feels like a lost little girl when men criticize her or threaten to end the romance. But she tends to stay in such relationships to "get it right" and prove to herself (on an unconscious level, at least) that her father had been wrong and that she was indeed lovable and worthy of a man's time and commitment. Jessica told me that, "When my father left, I think there was a part of me that determined never to feel that painful way again: to distance myself, to people-please, to manipulate and lie and to never feel that pain of abandonment again. In lots of ways, the pattern of my eating behavior has served to numb me from the pain of my father's leaving me when I needed him so badly. Today I can see the insanity of this logic—acting out addictively to numb my feelings of loss and rejection—but it made huge sense to me at the time."

Our self-esteem, identity, and self-confidence all stem from our childhood and adolescent years—and without a good foundation in these areas, we'll always be searching for satisfaction outside of ourselves, unless we are naturally wired to be resilient, find better role models, or learn new things about ourselves. Psychologists like Erik Erikson discovered the developmental stages in which a person basically "downloads" the cognitive and emotional framework that enables the brain to grow, and from which our adult personality is formed. Erikson's initial conceptualization of the stages of psychosocial development described eight stages through which a healthily developing human should pass from infancy to late adulthood. In each stage, the person confronts and, ideally, successfully masters its particular challenges. In the early stages, we form healthy or unhealthy need for love, approval, and validation. "The problem of adolescence is one of role confusion—a reluctance to commit which may haunt a person into his mature years. Given the right conditions—and Erikson believes these are essentially having enough space and time, a psychosocial moratorium, when a person can freely experiment and explore—what may emerge is a firm sense of identity, an emotional and deep awareness of who he or she is."[2] We know now that a sense of identity may take some people a lifetime if ever to actually discover. Is it any wonder then that if a troubled sexually confused teenager begins using drugs and alcohol to cope with confusion, it may always be an underlying problem well into adulthood? In this regard, why then would you label a teenager as powerless, diseased, or an addict?

When we don't receive the love, approval, and validation we need in our formative years, we experience cognitive dissonance—the tension that's created by having two opposing ideas or thoughts that conflict with one another. Cognitive dissonance occurs when people lack consistency in the quality of their thinking—and thus contradictory beliefs create frustration and confusion. It's the difference between what you think the world is and what the world actually is. For example, Maria is a beautiful, lingerie model who appears confident and happy. But Maria's internal dialogue may tell her she's overweight, emotionally needy, and dumb. This conflict makes Maria feel insecure and experience low self-esteem—thereby producing anxiety and depression. Her goal then becomes finding ways to reduce that inner tension. For example, she may text her boyfriend thirty times a day, or binge eat and then make herself vomit, or use drugs or alcohol excessively.

Maria is emotionally unstable and chooses to use certain behaviors to cope. But that doesn't mean she has a "disease" for which she needs to be medicated. This is her own personal subjective experience that she now needs to explore on a deeper level. By being mindful and making the associations of past learning with her present distress she can rethink those experiences and come to understand how they contribute to her preoccupation with love and approval. Maria may well have been given a "free pass" for most of her life because of her beauty and gained attention for it—but not the satisfaction she desires because her needs are constant. She learned early on that she could somewhat control and manipulate her environment to survive by her appearance. This became a false self. By being aware and understanding that her perceived underlying problems were learned, she'll realize that she must improve upon the quality of her thinking in order to dissipate the emotional attachment she has to people and things. From this, she'll reinforce her autonomy and develop more self-efficacy. Maria can then rely on her own coping skills and not need addictive behaviors or constant approval from others to make her life fulfilling and satisfying. This truer self will be more authentic and have power and an independent voice.

Social media and the numerous dating sites provide people with a strong need for feeling relevant. The more technology we have making communication easier and access to more people quicker and more efficient comes at a price: disconnection. Relationships, love, approval, and validation from images and text messages create a false sense that what they have to say or how they look is really important to thousands of other "friends" or "followers"—most of whom they don't even know. These platforms exist mainly because many people want to feel that they're influential and significant to a mass audience—almost like being a celebrity—even if they're living in relative obscurity. While most people use these sites to stay connected to friends and family—which is a healthy and fun thing—for many others, it becomes the way they communicate to the world that they actually exist. The lonely guy or girl can now go on a social media or dating site and find people who want to be their friend or date them—but are these people really their friends in the true sense of the word? Social media has stolen away a lot of the human connection that we truly need, whether it involves hearing live music on a date, talking on the phone with a friend, or simply eating a meal with one's family. As connected as we are today and as quickly as we can now communicate with others, in reality, we are becoming more disconnected, alienated, and alone.

Many people are meeting through mobile apps and online dating sites, in which often misleading photos and bogus personal profiles are posted to elicit a positive response. At their best, these channels offer the opportunity to meet multiple candidates and thereby increasing one's chances of finding a good romantic match or hook up. At least that is the intention. On the flip side, people who are emotionally manipulative, narcissistic, or want to take advantage of others financially or otherwise know that many users of these sites are emotionally vulnerable and susceptible to deception. More is not better. But for someone searching for love out of desperation and necessity these channels can become temporarily reinforcing with hope and a perception of being loved, approved, and validated.

Unfortunately, having intense experiences with hurtful individuals usually have a negative effect on someone's self-esteem, but ironically, people will continue to behave in patterned and predictable ways. We live in an age in which technology has taken us away from that human, personal bond we all require to be emotionally healthy. If we didn't get that validation from our primary caregivers, as adults we'll settle for a reasonable facsimile that never satisfies our true need. Contemporary technology is actually contributing more to our collective feelings of alienation and isolation than most people realize. More than ever, people today are starving for love, approval, and validation. Those with addictive behaviors are forming relationships in an attempt to satisfy their emotional needs. Thus, a person is prone to misinterpret lust for love, sex for commitment, fun for seriousness, and fantasy for reality. They're more prone to anxiety and depression, requiring something to help them through each day. Therefore, the learned behavior continues.

A preoccupation with love, approval, and validation involves living in bondage to what other people think and say about you. When you become obsessed with how others see you, no matter how much attention you receive, it's never enough. Without more and more "fixes," you'll suffer painful withdrawal symptoms when your "drug" of choice is withheld. Individuals who struggle with this problem often have no capacity to accept criticism. They hide from it, internalize it, or even become aggressive toward its originators. When what other people think of you becomes the organizing principle of your life, your entire identity is always on the line. An identity that is built upon a false self. You end up giving people access to your heart and mind who shouldn't have that access. You start to become what other people think of you, and after a while, the only thing that matters is how they perceive you. Validation will act to provide social proof, a psychological phenomenon in which people will mimic the actions of others in an attempt to reflect approved behavior in particular situations.

Social proof is a type of conformity. People who are not sure of themselves lose their independent voice. We are conditioned by our biology, family, culture, environment, and the social forces that influence our thoughts, feelings, and beliefs. This teaches us how to act in a situation by looking to others for the expected behavior. We often learn to make assumptions that others possess greater knowledge about what's expected, true, and normal. The effects of this social influence can be seen in the tendency of people in large groups to conform to choices which may be either correct or erroneous—a phenomenon sometimes referred to as groupthink, a common occurrence at AA's twelve-step group meetings.

Although social proof reflects the logical desire to take into account the information possessed by others, further examination shows that it can cause people to agree too quickly upon a single choice (for example, the cornerstone ideas of personal powerlessness, the disease model of addiction, and the need for lifelong recovery that are preached at AA meetings) so that decisions of even large groups of individuals may be grounded in very little verifiable information. Social proof often leads not only to conforming to the behavior of others without necessarily believing it's correct, but also subverts your own independent voice.

For example, this situation can be seen when an abstinent person in AA decides to begin drinking again after someone in the AA circle of friends has done so. Of course, she knows deep down that she isn't really powerless over her actions—but when her friend "goes out," using the excuse of personal powerlessness, then returning to drinking too by rationalizing that, "Well, then I guess I'm powerless too," is easy to do. But it's nothing more than a convenient excuse.

An extreme example of social proof has been proposed as an explanation for "copycat" suicide among teens—in which suicide rates tend to increase following news and social media publication about suicides.[3] One study showed that copycat suicides are more likely when there are similarities between the person involved in the publicized suicide and the potential copycats.[4] Loneliness, alienation, and failing to receive love, approval, and validation from key figures during formative years no doubt contribute to these tragedies. When we're denied the acceptance of others, or ignored by an important peer group, we may react to this interference due to our need to belong with anxiety, depression, and even rage. Being dependent upon love, approval, and validation from others for our sense of identity, self-esteem, and importance means that we must ceaselessly work at getting immediate gratification. We can never let up—because even if we gain the love and approval we're seeking, it can always be withdrawn.

We all need love and physical contact. We can't thrive without it, and in some cases, such as with newborns, we can't survive without it. However, problems occur when as adults we're still dependent on others as our primary source of love and attention. As long as we hold others responsible for defining our self-worth and making us feel safe and loved, we're likely to continue to feel lonely and empty inside.

Many people with low self-esteem have learned in therapy to verbalize self-affirmations such as, "I'm lovable" or "I'm worthy"—yet gain no positive results from such efforts. Why? Because when we recite self-approval mantras designed to positively "program" our unconscious mind, it is not enough to produce change unless it is emotionally experienced and demonstrated through behavior. We know that we're just "making it up," so the feeling self—involving our self-talk—lacks faith in positive mantras. Our self-talk will be especially skeptical if we continue to treat ourselves in self-abandoning ways—such as by harshly judging ourselves, ignoring our feelings, and turning to addictive behaviors for temporary relief.

But it doesn't have to be this way. What if you were to decide to give yourself the love, approval, and validation that you seek from others? What if you were determined to stop focusing externally about what you need from others and instead committed yourself to focusing internally? We all have the power to define our self-worth. You may think that the only love that feels truly satisfying must emanate from another person, but this isn't true at all. We all need approval. But too often we end up depending upon others for it, when what we really need to do is give it to ourselves first. Since excessive habits and addictive behaviors are examples of someone that has learned that the world revolves around them and their problems, challenges, and expectations, a good discipline to develop is learning to be mindful and self-compassionate. When you learn to be kinder to yourself you will be kinder, more compassionate, and empathetic toward others. When you present yourself in this way, the quality of your thoughts and beliefs will be different. When you think in this way you will be communicating more effectively and listening more attentively. You will be more humble, grateful, and appreciative. You will be more caring, genuine, and authentic. Ultimately, this is the love to seek.

5

RETHINKING EXCESSIVE HABITS AND ADDICTIVE BEHAVIORS

Excessive habits and addictive behaviors are normal human experiences and better understood as learning disorders that lie along a continuum. Hence the single-minded treatment approach of AA's twelve-step programs doesn't factor in each individual's unique circumstances. Rather than label everyone the same simply because they meet observable socially constructed criteria, the goal should be to deconstruct this emotionally charged deficit-based language. Indeed, it actually hinders self-discovery of the actual contributing influences for these types of behaviors by assigning little value to a thorough exploration of learning and ignoring the stories people tell themselves about themselves which is part of their subjective experience. Labeling someone as being diseased and powerless is self-fulfilling. Labels instill fear. Fear is inhibiting and has a destabilizing emotional hold over someone. Convinced by the group that one drink will lead to a complete downward spiral, many AA and twelve-step-indoctrinated individuals learn to binge-drink or otherwise act out addictively once they've "fallen off the wagon," as a way of proving to themselves and others (who would hold them accountable for their bad behavior) that they're indeed powerless. This is faulty reasoning. Failure to remain completely abstinent is always viewed as the individual's fault, never as a sign of the treatment philosophy's limitations. Therefore the standard AA and twelve-step response to a "relapse," which is also a normal human experience, is to insist that the individual attend more meetings, "work the steps" more diligently, and more actively help newcomers.

> Jon is a twenty-five-year-old computer technician who was sent to counseling because he came to work inebriated one day. Jon explained that he was just having fun at lunchtime, he understood it wasn't appropriate behavior during work hours, and that alcohol wasn't a problem for him. The counselor retorted that Jon was "in denial" and that his behavior was actually a symptom of a disease. Since Jon had to attend the counseling sessions to keep his job, he reluctantly agreed to acknowledge he had a drinking problem. This viewpoint was then reinforced at Jon's mandated AA meetings, where he has to subscribe to the idea that he was an alcoholic and powerless to change his incurable disease on his own.

> Nicole is a ninety-eight-pound college student in her early twenties who has consumed alcohol on only a few occasions in her life. One night, she goes out with friends to a club and consumes three drinks within an hour. Feeling disoriented by this new experience and not realizing she's had too much to drink too soon for her body weight, she makes the wrong decision to drive herself home. On Nicole's way home, she is pulled over at a roadside police check. Registering a blood alcohol count of over 0.08, she's arrested for DUI. Nicole was then mandated to AA where she's verbally coerced into admitting that she's an alcoholic, diseased, and powerless. This experience actually contributed to Nicole becoming noncompliant. Her noncompliance was seen as her reluctance to accept that she had a drinking problem.

In 2012, the National Center on Addiction and Substance Abuse at Columbia University (CASA), released a report concluding that, "only a small fraction of individuals receive interventions or treatment consistent with scientific knowledge about what works." Much of addiction treatment, the study asserted, could possibly be described as "a form of medical malpractice. Addiction treatment facilities and programs are not adequately regulated or held accountable for providing treatment consistent with medical standards and proven treatment practices."[1] Anne M. Fletcher, an award-winning science journalist and author of *Inside Rehab*, argues that many of CASA's findings are valid. Fletcher spent five years researching the effectiveness of traditional treatment in

America by talking to former patients of rehab facilities, as well as to employees who work there—and found that a core problem is their one-size-fits-all approach. She comments, "Alcoholics, drug addicts, the suicidal, anorexics, even video game addicts are all thrown in together, the prevailing wisdom being that the addiction may differ but the recovery process is the same."[2]

Addiction psychiatrist Dr. Mark Willenbring, a former director of the Division of Treatment and Recovery Research at the National Institute on Alcohol Abuse and Alcoholism (NIAAA), a government-funded organization, likewise remarked, "I keep coming across patient after patient who has been through rehab with either no benefit or with negative effects. It's atrocious that this is allowed to continue."[3] A. Thomas McLellan, PhD, a University of Pennsylvania psychiatry professor who has studied addiction for more than thirty years stated in regards to how rehabs primary rely on twelve-step meetings "if that doesn't work they'll try . . . 'group.' And when all else fails they'll suggest . . . 'group'!"[4] What he is referring to is, no matter the setting, at a rehab or a gathering at an AA meeting, the same myopic, dogmatic, and generalized information is being disseminated.

AA was formed for the purpose of helping individuals recover from severe drinking problems. AA has saved thousands of peoples' lives who would otherwise have nowhere else to go and this is unquestioned. Although I don't advise people to attend AA and other twelve-step groups, I'd never discourage anyone from doing so if it could be beneficial. Yes, if you're gaining real solutions to your problems at AA and twelve-step meetings, keep going. But, I believe if you are making the conscious behavioral choice to stop drinking and you believe it is because of the support and friendships you have gained by attending AA meetings, this is proof of your individual power not powerlessness. With an AA meeting on every block, someone in need of support can find a place to go rather easily and affordable. With such an already established built-in network, if AA progressed beyond their fundamental principles to adapt to a changing world, their contribution to helping people would be much greater. However, statistics show that AA and twelve-step is "effective" and appropriate based solely on the objective of people remaining abstinent. The statistic is generally stated to be around 5–8 percent who actually remain in AA for at least a year.[5]

Not long after Prohibition was repealed, AA was founded in 1935 and has remained essentially unchanged ever since. Over the ensuing decades, many other twelve-step programs have formed to help people experiencing difficulty with drugs, overeating, gambling, shopping, personal debt, and sex to name a few—and *all* of these behaviors are described as a "disease" by their respective groups. Although the disease model concept for all of these behaviors is culturally indoctrinated through mass media, the judicial system, and standardized education, most people quit "addictions" on their own with no outside treatment. This is why I believe redefining the word "addiction" is necessary. The language of the rehab industry is outdated. The only thing we must stop drinking is the Kool-Aid. Change the language and we will change behavior.

My father smoked Camel cigarettes for fifty years. In every sense of the contemporary language of addiction, he was dependent on nicotine physically and psychologically. After my father survived a heart attack his doctor urged him to stop smoking. What did my father do? He stopped immediately and never smoked again. Nor did he transfer his nicotine dependency by developing another type of addictive behavior. Now, whether implied or not, if the perception is that addiction is a disease and my father was addicted to nicotine, he had two diseases. Heart disease and an addiction to nicotine. He made the conscious choice to finally change his behavior through his actions because he wanted to. He was motivated on his own by this health scare and his desire to live for his family. The question then arises, had my father been given a brain scan prior to quitting, what would it have looked like? What would it have looked like after he quit? In other words, if his brain scan were to show that certain areas lit up and his addictive behavior was changing his brain, what happened when he stopped smoking? Did his brain not light up anymore? Did his brain change back to normal? This is an example of why using a word like disease is misleading and not useful. My father never smoked again and never transferred his former addictive behavior to something else. He simply chose to stop. The profound words of advice from Tim Robbins's character in the movie *The Shawshank Redemption* say it best: "my father had a choice to either 'get busy living or get busy dying.'" He chose life. This is a choice all people make when they are involved in self-sabotaging behaviors.

Historically, research on addiction mainly focused on alcohol. Ironically, despite AA releasing almost no information concerning its effectiveness (again, only meaning days remaining abstinent), a giant conceptual leap assumes that the AA and twelve-step treatment approach can be directly applied to drug use, sexual conduct, gambling, Internet use, eating, shopping—or any other excessive behavior, to warrant the disease label. We're culturally indoctrinated to think AA and twelve-step programs are the only way to treat these types of behaviors because the highly profitable treatment industry hasn't changed in many years and the mass media rarely inform the public about new research and developments. Despite numerous studies uncovering vital information about the positive application of alternative approaches, a gap has remained between science and practice.

Another fact worth mentioning is that when AA was formed in the 1930s, it wasn't intended for women or minorities. Hence, in a world of cultural diversity, progress, and inclusion, the fundamental targeted member is a white male. Until the early 1990s, most research on substance abuse and dependence focused almost exclusively on men. That situation changed significantly once federally funded studies were mandated to enroll more women.[6]

Better professional recognition of such gender differences should aid women in avoiding the pitfalls of substance use disorders, and also help addiction specialists and treatment facilities modify their approaches accordingly. Research shows that many women with addictive behaviors have trauma from past sexual or physical abuse. They're already feeling powerless and AA and twelve-step meetings often reinforce that negative feeling—a situation which causes these groups to be particularly inappropriate, ineffective, and potentially harmful for women.

The notion that addiction is a disease has its roots in the American Temperance Movement of the 1830s and 1840s. Then, most American males over the age of fifteen drank three times as much alcohol as we do today. Women had few legal rights and were dependent financially on men. When men got intoxicated, they often acted inappropriately toward women, became embroiled in fistfights with other men, and caused public disturbances. At the time, organizations were being formed to proclaim that such behaviors caused by intoxication were basically "the work of the devil." The demonization of alcohol in our society began, and it's still with us today. This is part of old-school thinking.

The idea of admitting powerlessness to reclaim some semblance of normalcy from an addictive behavior is not rational. I work with many highly functional people—who make major decisions daily, who are responsible for hundreds of people's livelihoods, and who are constantly problem solving and conflict resolving. Yet, they came to me with a belief that their drinking problem was something very different—in which their intelligence, common sense, and abilities were somehow rendered helpless. This is an absurd viewpoint.

Again, remember that AA was intended for the worst-case alcoholics, who were destroying themselves by liquor. Telling them they were in denial or powerless was justifiable if for no other reason than that it saved these people's lives back when little was known about treating alcohol-related problems. But, for the majority of people today, none of this applies anymore. The only thing you are denying is that your life circumstances and challenges may be getting the best of you—and that you need to examine what is really occurring with your subjective experiences.

It has become a disturbing trend to see so many well-known people being treated with an abstinence only–based approach tragically die of an overdose shortly after leaving rehabs. Or how you will hear about someone attending support groups for years for one problem only to be seriously involved with other unhealthy behaviors.

What twelve-step programs, powerlessness, and disease-belief have in common is a deficit-based mindset predicated on a conversion experience. Conversion experiences occur when someone is in a vulnerable and susceptible state of mind. This is why many people liken AA to being similar to a religion. Let me give you a real-life example. One year I volunteered to help serve meals to the homeless in downtown Los Angeles during Thanksgiving. The organization was a Christian nonprofit that held these events yearly during the holiday season. To me this was a wonderful thing and I did not care who was behind the event. After literally hundreds of homeless people who had waited for nearly an hour in the hot sun were eventually seated, another hour and a half would pass as they sat in the hot sun waiting to eat. Why? Because as part of providing the food came an agenda—ninety minutes of proselytizing. In essence, you will eat because Jesus is your savior, now come and get your bible. I am not wanting to be cynical. I think helping anybody in need is a good thing. The homeless situation in this country is a disgrace. Homeless shelters and missions are mainly supported by religious organizations. But I observed how these homeless people just needed to eat. Had I been running the event, I would have seen to it that eating was the first priority and then offered the opportunity to learn more about Jesus to anyone who desired afterward.

What I've found that AA and twelve-step programs do effectively is to take all the responsibility away from individuals, convince them that they're powerless to control their choices, and assure them that they are (as stated in AA's *Big Book*), "like men who have lost their legs and will never grow new ones."[7] Such a label provides members with an identity they've unconsciously been seeking as a way to deal with their emotional instability and suffering. The disease model as it's touted in AA and twelve-step programs strip people of their unique life experience and story, remove their personal responsibility, and label them identical to all the other powerless individuals in the group. These groups often interpret one's resistance to this definition as a symptom of a disease— asserting that the individual is arrogant to assume he is special or different by not wanting to be lumped with everyone else at meetings. One is told repeatedly that he isn't a unique individual and no different from other group members—possessing all the same "character defects" and "shortcomings"—and therefore the same problems. Yet this is simply not true.

What's even more damaging is the group practice in which members label themselves as "bodily and mentally different from their fellows." The normal majority is described as "normies." This conceptualization only reinforces feelings of isolation. Where did it originate? Although this comprises only a small percentage of the people with any drinking problem, this comes from studies of worst-case alcoholics. In effect, AA can be said to be appropriate for a small percentage of the people with serious drinking problems, because these are the individuals who have been in and out of jails, hospitals, and treatment institutions, and who are highly self-destructive. The friendships and support they gain by attending meetings, when and if contributing to their ultimate objective of abstinence is achieved, demonstrates clearly that they have made the conscious choice to stop voluntarily and that they possess a great deal of power.

But, what about the majority of people who may be having some difficulty related to their use of alcohol, drugs, or some other substance, but who aren't really dependent? The majority of these people aren't even medically viewed as having a substance use disorder or if they are, we know it lies along a continuum. Where do they go if they wanted to reach out for help? They're neither diseased nor powerless, but they often accept these stultifying labels because there's seemingly nowhere else to go.

A cultural change in the United States is imperative. We need to abandon the assembly-line approach to addictive behaviors and instead treat people appropriately for their specific situation. The addiction treatment industry has several dominant themes. One that manifests far too often is the tendency to blame the client for any treatment failure. It's customary for AA or a twelve-step treatment provider to put forth phrases like "He's still in denial" or "She didn't work the program" or "He hasn't hit bottom yet." It's assumed that any treatment failure inevitably reflects the individual's reluctance to submit to AA or twelve-step rigor, rather than to a weakness in the approach. Is noncompliance being in denial or any assertion of one's own autonomy? It's like going into an ice-cream shop and finding it sells one flavor: vanilla. We know there are many effective ways to help someone with addictive behavior. Most people want more "flavors" and would benefit from a competitive treatment marketplace in which a greater amount of education, media exposure, and government funding is allocated to research and treatment improvements. Not to maintain the status quo, but rather to change the language and raise the bar to intellectual curiosity and social discourse.

This situation can best be summarized by way of analogy. The United States is dependent on foreign and domestic oil—a situation creating myriad political and economic problems. Our country has an oil-dependent economy and is beholden to those who produce and control oil. Alternative fuels are not given priority even though they'd be better for the country in the long run. As long as we're dependent on this commodity that produces enormous financial gains for powerful corporations who control politicians, reasonable energy alternatives will be ignored or be accorded only lip service. The addiction industry operates in a similar way. AA and twelve-step treatments are the old commodities and new options are mostly ignored or marginalized by those who profit from the status quo. Unless voters force the government to set up an organization made up of mental health professionals who promote a variety of evidence-based treatments and alternative ways to rethink and change the language so that new theories and discoveries can be implemented for the benefit of all, little meaningful change in America will occur and the costs to society will continue to be felt not just economically, but in the psyche of the human spirit muted by self-surrender.

Oddly enough, you could say that while maintaining that alcoholism is a disease, AA, twelve-step programs, and other disease model proponents are ignoring ethically and responsibly to tell individuals of alternatives. Additionally, the AA and twelve-step philosophy rejects medical evaluation as part of its treatment regimen. The belief that alcoholism is a disease of the soul or spirit, rather than a physical disease like diabetes or cancer confuses matters for most people because these same individuals will be told by counselors and doctors they have a biological disorder. Which is it? A literal disease or an abstract one? Likely, the only reason the doctrine of powerlessness is preached in AA is because without the accompanying concept of a conversion experience, the notion that one is powerless would not have any purpose.

When AA cofounders Bill Wilson and Dr. Bob Smith first set out to help people, they had a friend rarely mentioned in AA literature: Tom Powers. In the beginning, these three men and others traveled in search of new recruits and made attempts to expedite the conversion experience central to the AA and twelve-step approach by taking hallucinogenic drugs. Even in its earliest days, the founders of AA were willing to try anything unconventional to produce a conversion experience. The creation of the twelve steps and reliance on God for healing came later.[8] I'm in no way criticizing religion or the idea of spirituality. But this dualistic approach of telling individuals they have a literal biological disease like cancer and need a support group to address their spiritual abstract disease is neither very useful nor logical. It is also confusing and counterintuitive.

Dr. Mark Willenbring, the former director of the NIAAA and who speaks the language of medicalized mental health disorders, discovered after conducting long-term studies on heavy drinkers that "although alcoholism can be a progressive brain disease, the majority of the time it is not. Therefore, we need to rethink what we know about heavy drinking."[9] What does he mean by "alcoholism can be a progressive brain disease"? Like anything you do to excess you risk harming your body. You could die from drinking too much water. He cited research which found that the majority of people who met the criteria for alcohol dependence, in a one-year follow-up, were either in partial or full recovery. Many were still drinking moderately and were not in any treatment at all. This important finding challenges the notion that alcoholism is progressive or uncontrollable, and that a person's only options are abstinence and faith-based adherence.

All drinking behavior lies along a continuum in terms of severity. But anyone can get a DUI arrest after imbibing just a couple of drinks and that person would be considered diseased once entering the treatment system. Moreover, research by NIAAA found that 70 percent of those that had experienced a classifiable disorder were able to quit drinking or cut back to safe consumption patterns without treatment after four years or less.[10] Between the ages of twenty to twenty-five, many people engage in the collegiate tradition of binge-drinking on weekends, yet relatively few of those same individuals continue to drink in excess after graduation once they settle down into careers, committed love relationships, and raising children.

The studies of William R. Miller, who helped develop the evidence-based treatment technique known as motivational interviewing (which by the way is counterintuitive when used in conjunction with the twelve-step approach), and his colleagues at the University of New Mexico reviewed the "effectiveness" of alcohol treatment approaches nearly forty years. One of his conclusions was that the traditional treatments which are mandated by the courts and used in the majority of U.S. treatment facilities are either the least effective or have little supporting research to validate their use. He found that the notion of relapse was predictive with these traditional treatments because participants were convinced that they had a disease and lacked coping skills.[11]

Regardless of what leads an individual to seek treatment in the first place, everyone needs to have their independence reinforced. The notion of suppressing growth and curiosity through deficit-based language hinders people from experiencing their autonomous voice. If someone is drinking excessively because of unresolved childhood trauma, AA purists would likely suggest to the distressed individual to forget the past, move on, and focus on remaining abstinent. But forgiveness and empathy are achieved only by being exposed to new ideas and behaviors that induce fundamental growth and change. When someone enters treatment experiencing cognitive and emotional distress, being able to truly forgive and move on in the AA or twelve-step treatment setting is unlikely. Why? Because rethinking and reframing past experiences and discovering underlying problems is accorded minimal priority in this approach. The dynamics of conformity found in AA and twelve-step meetings maintain life distress for many people, and thereby act as a contributory cause of dependent thinking. Without learning new things and improving upon the quality of thinking neither forgiveness nor emotional growth can take place.

The word "relapse" is an important word to rethink, redefine, or stop using. Conventional treatment for alcoholism often conceptualizes relapse as an equivalent to treatment failure. Logic assumes that the way a problem is conceptualized and defined will not only determine what solutions will be attempted, but will also define the client/patient. Instead of the view that remaining abstinent is proof of treatment success and individual noncompliance as proof of failure, it is better to state that no matter how individuals remain abstinent it is proof of their power to make choices and when they do not remain abstinent it is also proof of their ability to make choices. But is a relapse inevitably a return to problematic substance-related behaviors or can it also be an occasional indulgence? If an individual with a previous problem that resulted in an inability to function learns the necessary coping skills and determines how to control consumption without impairing functionality, is that really a relapse or failure of treatment? According to the AA and twelve-step-based approach the answer is "yes." To me, a return to reuse is a teaching moment. It's an opportunity to grow and evolve as a person when not viewed as a reason for doom and gloom.

Sharing in an AA and twelve-step meeting for the most part is limited to regurgitating AA dogma and strictly adhering to the AA group-think commandments of powerlessness, the need for lifelong recovery, and the certainty that this is an incurable disease. This largely means that a member could never share a story of hope that involved any other way of attaining positive changes in life, if it didn't conform to the strategies outlined in the "Big Book" of AA—the 1939 publication that members revere as if it were the Bible. Since members are discouraged from sharing underlying problems and positive ways they've discovered to address their problems that are not endorsed in the "Big Book," the nature of sharing is generally the rehashing of outdated recovery methods and familiar life experiences. This process reinforces the debilitating and deficit-based language which has been shaped, formed, and downloaded through learning.

The sponsor-sponsee relationship in AA and twelve-step groups is a curious dynamic, for it's a crucial part of the AA and twelve-step recovery approach. In essence, a new member who's dealing with an alcohol or substance use disorder which is accompanied by a degree of emotional distress, now is allowed under the premise of treatment to be counseled by another member who generally possesses no professional mental healthcare experience and who is by inference struggling daily to avoid cravings to drink or use drugs. These members often share an unconscious attraction for one another fueled by the reinforcement within a group setting. For example, many people will state that their sponsor and other group members have personality traits similar to their immediate family members or other significant people from a dysfunctional past.

Does this situation make good treatment sense? This obvious question seems to be lost among those who profit by using the language of relapse to suggest failure in the individual. The solution of course is to start all over again rather than learning from the experience and moving forward. The rehab industry could be renamed the relapse industry. Like prisons, which experience high rates of recidivism, so too do individuals whose only objective is to remain abstinent. Why? Because incarceration has been shown to teach an inmate how to be a criminal. Soon after their release, their best skills are criminally oriented. When patients leave rehab or any conventional treatment including AA attendance, they have learned to be powerless and shamed by personal failure if they began drinking or using again. The consequence? They begin drinking and using again. Who goes to rehab only once? What's the percentage of people who remain abstinent for long amounts of time? How many of these same people are experiencing positive well-being and satisfaction in all areas of their life?

Because the AA and twelve-step approach reinforces group conformity rather than individual autonomy, members rarely develop the coping skills required to deal with the life stressors that produced the need to act out addictively in the first place. By receiving a dual-diagnosis, essentially a person is stuck. They become dependent on the meetings and the focus on abstinence for the rest of their lives and the need to take pharmaceutical drugs for the rest of their lives. The implication is that anything other than compliance will adversely affect them when in reality this mindset of lost autonomy and self-surrender directly affects their subjective experience and positive well-being. Abstinence-only will not prevent cognitive and emotional problems, and without self-discovery and the reinforcement of your independent voice, it is more likely to exasperate the preconditions for the addictive behavior. Many people who remain abstinent from one behavior simply transfer it to other observable behaviors which include inappropriate displays of anger, unhealthy consumption of nicotine, sugar, and caffeine, sexual pursuit of vulnerable individuals, and many other still self-indulgent, self-destructive, and self-sabotaging behaviors which contribute toward maintaining the dependent mindset. Think about it logically. If you were to abstain from using alcohol but smoked two packs of cigarettes, gained too much weight from overeating, and came to rely upon pharmaceutical drugs to cope with your life challenges, how good is the quality of your thinking? How good is the quality of your subjective experiences? How good is the quality of your life? This quality can be observed by your behavior.

An effective group setting should allow people to be unique individuals while learning to solve their similar but not identical problems in their own way. There are no entrance requirements other than respectful interaction. Certainly, group members aren't required to define themselves based on the lowest and most vulnerable point of their lives. An individual's autonomy, intuition, and personal sense of right and wrong should provide guidance in making choices. Decisions shouldn't be made based on how the group defines reality—the ethos and dominant rule in twelve-step meetings.

AA and twelve-step meetings involve the sharing of mostly negative experiences. Feedback or "crosstalk" is forbidden. One of the best hopes for ethically sound group support for substance use disorders is for the ability to give and receive positive feedback in a safe, supportive environment. Like any solution-focused/problem-solving session, the objective should be to create or inspire a course of action that is right for the individual and not just an ideology forced upon them. The model group setting should encourage individuals to learn from each other in order to *correct* negative experiences of the past while teaching self-reflection, communication skills, and conflict-resolution techniques. The ideal outcome is for members to take the lessons learned in the group setting and apply these to their lives outside the group. This approach will empower them to grow and change independently, rather than remain dependent on the group for the rest of their lives.

We need to rethink the language. It's outdated. It's overused, misused, and emotionally charged. It reinforces the mindset of dependency. Rather than dictate with absolute certainty what is occurring in the mind of an individual whose subjective experiences are known only to them or make assumptions about brain functioning when nobody knows what is going on at any given moment in someone's brain let's support the reinforcement of an individual's independent voice. Let's be kinder, nonjudgmental, and empathetic. Let's encourage new learning. Let's appreciate an individual's conditioned response to their environment. Let's teach mindfulness and self-compassion. We know today that treatment approaches like brief interventions, social skills training, motivational interviewing, and cognitive behavioral therapy produce positive outcomes by encouraging and supporting personal responsibility and choice. By deconstructing the socially constructed ideology of the conventional language used in the treatment industry, and rethinking, reframing, or removing the old-school vocabulary, I believe more people will be open and receptive to help-seeking.

6

DECONSTRUCTING DEFICIT-BASED LANGUAGE

No scientific evidence exists that proves "addiction" is a literal disease. The use of the term is purely a social construction and metaphorical. Nearly forty years of research has failed to uncover a missing gene, a chemical imbalance, or even a bodily allergy to prove that addiction is a literal disease. Nothing has been found. No medical tests confirm that addictive behavior is a literal disease, even though it's often compared by mainstream professionals to diabetes and cancer, illnesses that can be confirmed with a blood test. Social scientists have suggested that the concept of addictive behavior as a disease is based more on historical, social, and cultural factors than on actual medical discoveries. Reliable evidence suggests that this is a socially constructed concept used to standardize the multibillion dollar pharmaceutical drug and treatment and rehab industries.

> Robert is a forty-eight-year-old builder who has been smoking cigarettes for thirty years. He smokes a pack a day and is psychologically and physically dependent on them. If we accept the theory that addictive behavior is a disease, then we'd say that Robert is diseased. Scientists and addiction specialists agree that nicotine is one of the hardest drugs to quit—some say even harder than heroin. After a severe bout with bronchitis, Robert's physician advises that he should no longer smoke. Robert now makes the conscious behavioral choice to quit cigarettes "cold turkey" and never smokes again— without any treatment whatsoever.

Lynn self-administers enough morphine to kill several people during her stay in intensive care for advanced cancer. She has built up an enormous tolerance and has become physically dependent on the drug, which is a legally prescribed pain-killer used in hospitals. After returning home, Lynn weans herself off morphine when she and her physician decide she no longer requires it for pain.

On the flip side, Denise has recently been using heroin, which is chemically the same drug as morphine. But heroin is illegal. This makes its use socially unacceptable. Denise is using heroin to deal with the emotional pain and trauma she has felt for years after an abusive childhood. Just like Lynn, Denise is self-administering what is essentially the same drug. But when Denise goes to rehab for assistance in freeing herself from heroin, she's advised that she has a disease and is a drug addict.

The language used in conventional addiction treatment can be said to be verbally abusive. This prevalent situation limits treatment options and lumps everyone together in a cost-effective, single-minded approach. However, for the most part, such an orientation fails to take individual human experience into account. Human experiences can incorporate the learned use of a variety of substances and behaviors to cope with one's life challenges. When these experiences become problematic, they typically encompass craving for a particular substance or behavior, an inability to control it, and continued use despite severe negative consequences. Dependence on a substance over time—typically for a year or longer—is marked by greater tolerance for the substance, loss of control over its use, and less focus on other meaningful activities or commitments. Abuse describes people who use a substance excessively on a regular basis despite endangering themselves, jeopardizing their relationships, and failing on major responsibilities—but who don't yet manifest signs of dependence, such as a psychological compulsion or a physical need to use the substance. Since these human experiences look similar but are not identical, and because these behaviors vary in their causes, duration, and severity, I believe it is useful to rethink addictive behaviors in terms of a learning/spectrum in reality of the human condition.

For professionals to gain control of this reality, labeling someone with a disease has limited utility for the individual. It is more useful to view someone who has learned to become dependent on substances and behaviors as masking the distress created by chaotic and undisciplined thinking. In addition, poor choices are a byproduct of poor thinking and automatic stored learning responses which are void of the coping skills necessary to deal with the current life challenges in daily living. No book on treating addictive behavior in the United States would be complete without understanding from the outset that, even within the medical community, confusion reigns concerning how words like alcoholism, addiction, and disease are used. I believe this language is outdated.

For example, the word "addiction" is emotionally charged. It generally refers to the physical and psychological aspects of substance use—such as preoccupation, craving, tolerance, withdrawal, and a disregard for the consequences resulting from negligent behavior. This is a problematic viewpoint, because the same language is used to define and treat other human experiences that do not involve substances. At the same time, would the morphine user in the hospital setting be considered a drug addict and diseased for using this drug daily? Of course not. Unfortunately, many mental health professionals use the words addiction and disease interchangeably to encompass all substance use disorders and all behaviors that have been deemed socially inappropriate even when the word itself can be harmful. Furthermore, it's crucial to understand that the word "disease" has a broad meaning and its usage accommodates medical professionals by expanding its significance to serve their own interests.

All people are susceptible to addictive behavior as they find ways to cope with their problems in living. As times change people experience more and more stressors and distractions. For instance, people nowadays can become preoccupied with social media—which they couldn't not too long ago. If a person is addicted to texting, does he have a disease? Was the genetic tendency inherited from a parent? Logically, none of this makes sense. But the language is still in use with no clarification or differentiation.

The idea of addictive behaviors as a disease gained a tentative foothold in scientific and government circles in the early 1960s, after the publication of E. M. Jellinek's book *The Disease Concept of Alcoholism.* Jellinek may not have invented the "alcohol science movement" as he called it, and he may not have been much of a scientist himself, but he was the first to describe the "disease syndrome" of alcoholism—chronic relapse leading to death by liver failure. A salesperson by personality, Jellinek ardently presented the disease model of alcoholism to the world of the social sciences. The trouble was that the "science" part of alcohol science was murky at best. Jellinek had little scientific proof to support his contention, but that didn't seem to matter.[1] Already central to AA's influential view of alcoholism as a disease, Jellinek's notion was enthusiastically promoted by America's growing treatment industry—and then expanded in the 1960s and 1970s to address a variety of individual problems ranging from drug addiction and gambling to overeating and sexual adventurism. For over twenty-five years, the unitary disease model of alcohol dependency has been found scientifically shaky—with even less reliable data to support its extension to other addictive behaviors.

As an example of celebrity culture and the misuse of language was the situation concerning Tiger Woods's stay years ago at the Pine Grove rehab facility in Mississippi. After the discovery that he had been having several dalliances in spite of being married, he was sent to Pine Grove, for what mainly became damage control to his image. This facility which is run by physicians and treats, as their website stated at the time, "Those suffering from sexual addiction, relationship addiction, and sexual anorexia." If Woods had been unmarried would his behavior have made it necessary for him to seek treatment for the "disease of sex addiction"? Obviously if you're married, then having sex with anyone else is a betrayal of your spouse, and if you're unmarried, then engaging in sex with multiple partners is probably not a good idea. But in either case is the behavior indicative of a disease? What if Tiger Woods had been single? Would he now be viewed with a problem? As a society we fear the unknown and always seek out certainty. How can someone with a beautiful wife and children and is rich, famous, and successful behave in such a way? He must be suffering from a disease. He had no choice in the matter.

When reviewing the prevailing approaches to treatment, the way a problem is defined will affect how it's dealt with. The disease theory is based upon the idea that addiction causes physical changes in the brain and related to the reward system which is rich in the pleasure neurotransmitter dopamine. However, dopamine is released when enjoying anything pleasurable like eating, exercising, engaging in sex, or listening to your favorite music. These behaviors also change the brain physically from moment to moment. Everything we think, feel, and do changes the brain. Dopamine is released in the brain all day long. We know through neuroplasticity that the brain can rewire itself. We must differentiate from actual genetic defects, brain damage due to trauma, short- and long-term changes of intoxication and habituation. Dopamine and dopamine receptors do not prove cause. They may be useful theories and some theories are more useful than others, but they are not absolutes, simply biological reductionism.

Dr. Carl Hart is a neuroscientist at Columbia University. In his new book *High Price*, he describes his work with "addicts" seemingly enslaved by crack cocaine—people who, not unlike laboratory rats, couldn't stop "pressing the lever" for crack even as they were destroying their lives. The crack was providing such a powerful dopamine stimulation to the brain's reward center that the addicts just couldn't resist taking another hit. At least, that was how the situation appeared to Dr. Hart when he started his research.

Like many other scientists, Dr. Hart hoped to find a neurological cure for addiction: a way to block the dopamine activity in the brain so that people wouldn't give in to the otherwise irresistible craving for cocaine, heroin, and other powerfully addictive drugs. But when he began studying addicts more closely, he saw that using drugs wasn't so uncontrollable after all. "Eighty to ninety percent of people who use crack and methamphetamine don't get addicted," declares Dr. Hart. He conducted experiments in which test subjects were offered money instead of more crack after they had received an initial dose of the drug. Sometimes the reward was $5 in cash, and other times it was a $5 voucher they could redeem at a store. When their dose of crack was fairly high, the subjects would typically choose to keep smoking crack during the day. But when their dose was smaller, they were more likely to refuse it for the $5 cash/voucher.

"They didn't fit the caricature of the drug addict who can't stop once he gets a taste," Dr. Hart comments. "When they were given an alternative to crack, they made rational economic decisions." He also found that when he raised the alternative reward to $20, every single addict chose the cash. Even though they knew they wouldn't receive it until the experiment ended weeks later, they were still willing to refuse an immediate high.[2]

Based on such findings, Dr. Hart argued that the caricature of enslaved addicts comes from a misinterpretation of the famous rat experiments. "The key factor is the environment, whether you're talking about humans or rats," he notes. "The rats that keep pressing the lever for cocaine are the ones who are stressed out because they've been raised in solitary conditions and have no other options. But when you enrich their environment, and give them access to sweets and let them play with other rats, they stop pressing the lever." While some who subscribe to the disease model of addiction are skeptical of Hart's work, other scientists are impressed. "Carl's overall argument is persuasive and driven by the data," commented Craig R. Rush, a psychologist at the University of Kentucky who studies stimulant abuse. "He's not saying that drug abuse isn't harmful, but he's showing that drugs don't turn people into lunatics. They can stop using drugs when provided with alternative reinforcers."

A similar assessment comes from Dr. David Nutt, a British expert on drug abuse. "I have a great deal of sympathy with Carl's views," comments Nutt, a professor at Imperial College London. "Addiction always has a social element, and this is magnified in societies with little in the way of work or other ways to find fulfillment. It's much simpler for politicians and journalists to focus on the evils of a drug than to grapple with the underlying social problems." But Dr. Hart also puts some of the blame on scientists. "Eighty to ninety percent of people are not negatively affected by drugs, but in the scientific literature nearly one hundred percent of the reports are negative," he comments. "There's a skewed focus on pathology. We scientists know that we get more money if we keep telling Congress that we're solving this terrible problem. We've played a less than honorable role in the war on drugs."[3]

The dopamine theory of addiction is completely misleading. Many people are enamored with scientific research. But when the National Institute on Drug Abuse (NIDA) promotes the theory of the neurotransmitter dopamine and dopamine receptors as the *cause* of addiction, there are a few things that people should understand.[4] First, in scientific research, outcomes may be reliable, but not valid. Laboratory experiments on animals in controlled environments cannot be generalized to prove cause on complex subjective human experiences. How would chemically induced controlled animal experiments prove that human love, sex, alcohol, shopping, and problem gambling are caused by the same biological theory? Second, not all research is the same. When you have special interests funding studies to support a political and financial agenda is it any surprise that the majority of the news reports on new findings will be biased? We have become enamored with brain-imaging studies as the scientific support and validation for disease theories.

Yet, the field of interpersonal neurobiology theorizes that the brain is shaped and formed from social experiences and through the process of neuroplasticity. Therefore, one can change brain functioning by changing the way he thinks and believes. Furthermore, addictive behaviors involving eating, gambling, the Internet, shopping, romantic relationships, and a variety of other behaviors are just that, behaviors that are used as coping strategies to numb and mask emotional distress. Lastly, it's true that someone who becomes so preoccupied with an addictive behavior that she can no longer live a normal and productive life, obviously has a serious problem. It's also true that someone who becomes so preoccupied with an addictive behavior can learn to change these behaviors if they change the language used to define their human experiences.

Research psychologist Gene M. Heyman in his book *Addiction: A Disorder of Choice* has shown evidence that problematic drug users still demonstrate the ability to change their use to less problematic levels on their own. The suggestion being that addiction is not chronic, and although self-limiting, it involves choice. He states that addiction involves voluntary behavior. These voluntary behaviors are experienced as compulsions which are acted upon by contingencies.[5]

In a study published by the Ethics and Public Policy Center, Dr. Sally Satel, a staff psychiatrist at the Oasis Clinic in Washington, D.C., and lecturer in psychiatry at the Yale School of Medicine, observed that the findings of the brain disease model fail to include the "vocabulary of personhood and such words as responsibility, choice and character," and that "the fact that many, perhaps most addicts, are in control of their actions and appetites for circumscribed periods of time shows that they are not perpetually helpless victims of a chronic disease."[6]

Rehab counselors and self-appointed AA and twelve-step "gurus" caution new members that their disease is like diabetes or cancer. They don't suggest a more metaphoric use of the word as meaning something problematic of a voluntary choice in behavior, rather the label is meant to be literal. If you have cancer—a disease to which addictive behavior is often compared—you certainly don't need a physician who has had cancer and experienced chemotherapy or radiation too to help heal your body. You need a positive, well-educated physician who is knowledgeable about all the latest developments in research and treatment, someone who regards you as a unique individual with the ability to be the driving force in your own return to good health. Having somebody to directly identify with through similar life experience may be comforting, but it's not essential. What is required is a nonjudgmental, empathetic person who understands that language preceded behavior. If addictive behaviors are voluntary and involve choice, they can be voluntarily changed to nonaddictive behaviors involving choice.

Suffering is a part of the human condition. The challenge is to learn effective ways to make conscious behavioral choices through the language of our subjective experiences. It may be personally gratifying to be ten years sober in AA, but if you're still dealing with unresolved problems of anger or depression—and in seeking to avoid dealing with these emotions, you merely transfer your dependency to another addictive behavior like sexual promiscuity and justify it by insisting that you're abstinent from alcohol—all you've really done is changed how you cope with your unmet emotional needs by switching from alcohol dependency to excessive sexual behavior. What has not changed is the quality of your thinking.

An illustration of this pattern can be seen among many long-term AA members, who, despite being sober from alcohol for many years, continue to smoke. According to the Centers for Disease Control and Prevention (CDC), the adverse health effects from cigarette smoking account for an estimated 443,000 deaths per year—or nearly one of every five fatalities annually in the United States. CDC statistics find that: "More deaths are caused each year by tobacco use than by all deaths from AIDS, illegal drug use, alcohol use, motor vehicle injuries, suicides, and murders combined. Smoking causes an estimated 90% of all lung cancer deaths in men and 80% of them in women."[7] You will find individuals who attend AA and twelve-step-based support groups have a rate of smoking that's nearly twice as high as that of the general population. Many also freely consume large amounts of unhealthy sugar and caffeine. So if you're attending AA and twelve-step meetings, diligently working the steps with your sponsor, and you believe you're diseased and powerless to stop drinking or taking drugs on your own, then why wouldn't you use the same method to stop your habit of smoking that everyone knows actually will kill you? Bill Wilson, the cofounder of AA, died of the medically verifiable disease of emphysema—a lung condition directly related to excessive smoking. Back in his day, smoking was merely considered a minor vice. After all, unlike with alcohol dependency, nobody got into fistfights, car accidents, or acted inappropriately from smoking too many cigarettes. So, such addictive behavior became acceptable. Doctors even endorsed particular brands of cigarettes in television commercials until outlawed by federal legislation.

If you attend an AA meeting in most places throughout the United States today, you'll discover this transference of the problematic behavior to other things. Does it make sense that people would have no control over a daily habit of ingesting an addictive drug (nicotine via tobacco use) that's slowly killing them—while simultaneously attending meetings acknowledging that they're diseased and powerless over alcohol? I think not. Remember, alcohol or drug abuse refers to a maladaptive patterned use of a substance while drug use (as in, for example, recreational marijuana use) can be relatively harmless and in no way negatively impact the user. Nicotine and caffeine are addictive drugs that are legal and consumed on a mass scale. However, GHB, a naturally occurring substance in the central nervous system, is illegal to possess or consume in pharmaceutical form. The question always comes down to, "What is your relationship with this behavior?"

Statistics show that nearly twenty-three million Americans identify as having a substance use disorder but fewer than 10 percent seek treatment.[8] This finding suggests that some people who need help are reluctant to get it for reasons that relate to the type of treatment being offered or the lack of other options. Statistics show that 93 percent of the treatment available in the United States is AA and twelve-step-based which means that 100 percent of the people that are treated in these settings are taught to believe that they have a progressive, incurable disease over which they're powerless. If research shows that the disease model appears to be more of a historical and cultural construct rather than based on any scientific discoveries and that addictive behavior is voluntary and involves choice, it would suggest that the utility of the conventional language needs to be rethought. Changing the language will make help-seeking more desirable because people will come to understand that their self-destructive and self-sabotaging compulsions have been learned and so they can be unlearned. Once unlearned and replaced with new learning, they become new choices.

7

PHARMACEUTICAL DRUGS AND THE DSM-5

The diagnostic criteria for substance use disorders and many other mental disorders are classified in the American Psychiatric Association's current *Diagnostic and Statistical Manual* (DSM-5) and are often not based on scientific discoveries, but on the consensus of task forces of psychiatrists with direct financial ties to the pharmaceutical industry. The DSM-5 uses the term "addictive disorders" which is progressive. But the conventional language still uses the word "addiction" with all of its socially-indoctrinated implications. This is ironic since the multibillion dollar treatment industry has been using the term for decades and has generalized its use to a variety of behaviors. In so doing they are labeling people with disorders and treating them with drugs based primarily on misguided assumptions and financial incentives. There is a perception in this country with the American public that "drugs" are illegal and harmful and prescribed pills are medication and therefore good. The reality is drugs are drugs. Since the chemicals in the brain are always active, everything we think, feel, and do changes brain chemistry. But to suggest that there is a "chemical imbalance" in the brain with no way to test for what a chemical balance even is, is misleading, especially when it is the main justification for prescribing drugs. So when antidepressants like SSRIs are given to someone, if they work, it's allegedly because they increased serotonin in the brain. If these don't work, then other antidepressants are prescribed. This is conventional thinking. It's my opinion that the brain, prior to taking antidepressants, is normal—and that medication alters the brain and produces dependency. Antidepressant drugs increase suicidal ideation in many people and other side effects can be quite harmful too. Research shows that placebos are virtually as effective as antidepressant drugs when treating mild to moderate cases of depression.

> Sheila is a fifty-five-year-old woman whose husband of ten years recently died of cancer. She's told that because she's been sad for several months, she should be on an antidepressant drug. The drug makes Sheila lethargic and even more depressed. Now that bereavement can now be seen as an opportunity to prescribe medication, Sheila's subjective experience of dealing with her loss is made worse by her numbed feelings.

> Mark is a forty-year-old man who had been taking Seroquel for ten years. He weaned himself off the drug after learning that a large percentage of people taking it experienced liver damage. After a couple of weeks Mark stated that he felt like he had been rebooted. His senses were awakened, his mind was clear and his body felt renewed. His daily afternoon drinking routine lost its appeal and he regained a sense of control over his thoughts and emotions that he had not experienced while taking his "medicine."

In a May 2012 *New York Times* report regarding the recently released fifth edition of the American Psychiatric Association's (APA) DSM, the "bible" of the pharmaceutical industry which influences how most doctors in the United States treat their patients, Dr. Allen J. Frances, a professor of psychiatry and behavioral sciences at Duke University, stated that, "The overly broad and vaguely worded definitions in the new DSM-5 will create more false epidemics and cause increased medicalization of every day behavior."[1]

Dr. Lisa Cosgrove, a fellow at the Safra Center for Ethics at Harvard University added that, "The ties between the DSM-5 panel members and the pharmaceutical industry are so extensive that there is a real risk of corrupting the public health." A recent study published by Dr. Cosgrove reported that, "a full two-thirds of the manual's advisory task force members reported ties to the pharmaceutical industry or other financial conflicts of interest."[2]

When the first DSM came out in 1952, it was a thin, spiral-bound edition regarded as more of a guide to psychiatry than as a final authority on everything pertaining to mental health. Somehow, however, the DSM acquired that pretense in 1980, with the publication of the third edition—which included more than one hundred new mental disorders and switched diagnostic criteria to conform to the disease concept of illness and presenting symptoms. It was a clear shift from the former, Freudian approach to the new idea of chemical imbalances in the brain and how these could supposedly be treated with drugs. This new conceptualization was touted as "biological psychiatry" and embraced theories about neurotransmitters like serotonin and dopamine. Since psychiatrists are physicians and can prescribe medication, they began to control the entire mental health field and push out psychotherapy and counseling. By the early 1990s, this approach had come to dominate public policy and treatment strategy—from the federal government to educators, law enforcement officials, and medical facility and insurance administrators. Everything in diagnosis shifted to the lens of the disease model and the availability of drugs to treat symptoms. It was a facile, "one-size-fits-all" way of viewing and treating patients' problems.

Simultaneously, the pharmaceutical corporations began supporting financially many of the "studies" that physicians were citing to justify giving people drugs. For example, a DSM-4 personality disorders survey that was conducted for the World Health Organization—the results of which were published in 2009—was heavily funded by Eli Lilly, Ortho-McNeil, GlaxoSmithKline, and Pfizer, all pharmaceutical drug manufacturers.[3] In turn, psychiatrists were putting together the DSM's classifications of symptoms and disorders—not strictly by science or independent research studies, but by committee—with many of the people on these panels enjoying financial and other ties to the drug companies.

As of this day, no conclusive medical research concerning any of these disorders exists. Rather, a group of psychiatrists say *yes* or *no* to syndromes that are often invented to sell a drug for treatment. And so we're bombarded with "restless leg syndrome" and other unproven diseases that are conceptualized by committees. Because psychiatry has been unable to determine even a single medical cause for any mental disorder and the diagnoses lack scientific rigor, virtually anyone can be labeled mentally ill and subjected to dangerous and life-threatening treatments based solely on opinion and greed.

Dr. Harold Pincus, vice chairman of the DSM-4 task force has admitted, "There has never been any criterion that psychiatric diagnoses require a demonstrated biological etiology (cause)." Psychologist Renee Garfinkel, a staff member of the American Psychological Association, said of the DSM-3-R review committee: "The low level of intellectual effort was shocking. Diagnoses were developed by majority vote on the level we would use to choose a restaurant. You feel like Italian, I feel like Chinese, so let's go to a cafeteria. Then it's typed into the computer."[4]

The DSM now contains three times as many disorders as it did in 1952—and is more than seven times longer than the first edition. The proverbial jury is still out on whether the dozens of new "diseases and brain disorders" will actually hold up to scientific scrutiny. For example, "prolonged bitterness" was actually being viewed as a brain disorder— so if you moan incessantly that the federal government can't account for all the taxes it collects or about the sharp decline in your retirement account, you could have been considered mentally ill. Why? Because a small group of mental health professionals believes that you shouldn't think about such matters for too long. But the language is troubling because when you associate the word "addiction" to behaviors like Internet use, shopping, sexual activity, and shopping without differentiating the meaning with substance use and yet you define and treat in the same way, it creates more problems than it attempts to solve. How these task forces decide when normal complaining becomes a disorder—or when one's frequency of sex become excessive—is still anyone's guess. This is because the APA has no clear definition of the boundary between typical and pathological responses to life's problems.

An even more disturbing fact is that everyone involved in putting the DSM together must sign a contract promising not to share publicly what's going on behind closed doors. The contract reads in part that: "I will not, during or after the term of this appointment divulge, furnish, or make accessible to anyone or use in any way . . . any Confidential Information about the development process that emanates from or relates to my work with the APA task force."[5] Apparently the public is not supposed to ever know exactly how or why many human life experiences become mental disorders.

To its critics, the APA boasts that the manual is evidence-based, drawing on data and field trials. But the very fact that they've produced a task force to decide whether bitterness, apathy, extreme shopping, and overuse of the Internet belong in the manual indicates that the new edition of the DSM is flawed. Dr. Allen Frances, who also chaired the task force that produced the DSM-4 states in his criticism of the DSM-5 states, "unfortunately, the extensive research has had no effect on psychiatric diagnosis, which still relies exclusively on fallible subjective judgments rather than objective biological tests."[6] This is an astounding statement from a man who was partially responsible for overseeing the formal approval of more than 150 mental disorders in his former position with the APA. Conceivably, we might reach a point in the near future where the APA is defining more than half the country as mentally ill.

Psychiatry's 300 percent increase of mental disorders in the DSM over fifty years has already generated hundreds of billions of dollars in profits for pharmaceutical companies. Just since the DSM-4 was released in 1994, there has been a 256 percent increase in psychiatric drug sales.[7] Indeed, "despite 22 international regulatory warnings on psychiatric drugs citing effects of mania, hostility, violence and even homicidal ideation—and dozens of high profile shootings/killings tied to psychiatric drug use—there has yet to be a federal investigation into the link between psychiatric drugs and acts of senseless violence."[8]

Aren't you curious why not?

A September 2013 report from the Centers for Disease Control (CDC) found a massive rise in the overall rate of fatal painkiller overdoses from 1999 to 2010, a higher rate than the fatality rate of those who are consuming heroin and cocaine. Specifically, the rate of painkiller deaths is about four times higher overall than that from cocaine and heroin combined. The report stated that the death rate from prescription painkiller overdose rose 415 percent among women and 265 percent among men in those years. Officials with the CDC also found a five-fold increase in prescriptions for powerful painkilling medications, "but no similar increase in the incidence of painful conditions that warrant them."[9]

What this means is that as pharmaceutical drugs are more accepted in society as a way of dealing with life problems, we see an abundance of prescriptions being written for people—with virtually no increase in real medical conditions. The drug companies and the Food and Drug Administration (FDA) are entirely aware of this, so why are they still dosing up millions of patients with painkillers? Sure, it can be challenging to identify which individual patients need or do not need the drugs, but it's not hard to figure out that something might be wrong with promulgating millions of extra painkillers each year with absolutely no spike in real conditions. The drug industry is out of control and the socially accepted "legal" drugs are even more dangerous than the illegal ones. We have an entire population of legal drug users who are dying more often than even users of narcotics.

Moreover, antidepressant and other pharmaceutical drugs can be just as harmful to you physically or psychologically as any other substance that you put into your body—whether legally prescribed or not. Keep in mind, all chemicals affect your brain. Marcia Engel, who lectures at Harvard Medical School and was the first female editor in chief of *The New England Journal of Medicine* reported that since Prozac came out in 1987 the number of diagnoses for depression in the United States has tripled. Ten percent of Americans over the age of six are now on some type of antidepressant medication.[10] So what is actually happening here? Are we in a state of affairs in which we have drugs being created first and then problems being diagnosed or "invented" afterward?

Irving Kirsch, another Harvard Medical School lecturer, debunked the antidepressant myth in his book *The Emperor's New Drugs*. He conducted placebo studies and found that a placebo (which is basically a sugar pill made to resemble the actual drug to which it's being compared) was three times more likely to produce favorable results among participants compared to those who had received no treatment at all. The members of this group also showed improvements that were on par with those experienced by the group of test subjects who had been given the antidepressant drug itself.[11]

Think about that. If you were experiencing depression to a mild to moderate degree and knew that you could just "believe" you were taking a medication—and that this belief in and of itself would reduce your symptoms significantly—why would you spend the time and money to take a potentially dangerous drug? Sophisticated marketing and advertising make people think they *need* these medications. We learn to accept this as the reality. Pharmaceutical companies are some of the largest and richest corporations in the world—and the more drugs they can sell the more profits they earn. They don't care about your long-term health or your children's health—only about profits. Even if you have comprehensive health insurance, these drugs can be expensive and habit-forming. You're told you have a disease and a chemical imbalance. So you accept the whole line of thinking and become dependent. You go back to the pharmacy month after month for your refill. What do you call such behavior, especially when you may not even need the medication yet take it every day? This is more in line with being addicted. A person that is both psychologically and physically dependent on their daily drugs.

Kirsch has argued that the notion of a chemical imbalance in the brain is misguided at best. Remember, people who are taking antidepressant medications are taking these because they've been told that there is an imbalance of chemicals in their brain. They're assured that the antidepressant drug will produce the necessary balance in their brain, thus making them able to function. But even "therapeutic" levels of drugs require the brain to adapt. Therefore the changes in the brain are not corrective as much as they are disruptive. The general public has learned that their inability to cope with their life challenges can be compartmentalized simply by reducing all their problems to their faulty brain from which a daily regime of pills can fix the problems. That is the perception.

In *The Anatomy of an Epidemic: The Magic Bullet: Psychiatric Drugs and the Astonishing Rise of Mental Illness in America*, Robert Whitaker relates that neurotransmitter functioning (involving the chemicals in your brain that control mood and many other processes) seems to be normal in people with mental illness prior to treatment and that they only present abnormal brain functions during testing after they've taken antidepressant medications.[12] Based on this research, people who have depression are really just experiencing something that's distressing and they lack the coping skills to deal with it effectively. They could have lost a family member, experienced recent job loss, or gone through a painful romantic breakup. These major life stressors would make anyone feel anxious and depressed. We all have problems and experience pain in our lives. It's a normal part of the human condition. But what increasingly happens in the United States today is that people see a physician or therapist and are advised to try an antidepressant—and that really does alter the brain chemistry.

Once this situation occurs, the drug's side effects make you feel like you really do have a problem. But one is usually told to just continue to take the medication. Sometimes additional medications are prescribed to deal with the unwanted side effects of the first medication. Sounds counterintuitive, doesn't it? Even though we're talking about a legally prescribed drug from a doctor, you've now become a person dependent on a substance—just like a smoker is dependent on nicotine or an alcoholic on booze.

The psychiatrist Daniel Carlat, contended in *Unhinged: The Trouble with Psychiatry: A Doctor's Revelations about a Profession in Crisis*, that, "There is no such thing as a chemical imbalance in the brain that can be linked to behavioral or mental disorders and that in fact these 'diseases' have been socially constructed to fit a drug that was created by powerful pharmaceutical corporations focused mainly on profits."[13]

For example, research shows that people diagnosed with either depression or schizophrenia have lower levels of serotonin in their brain. Researchers then made the conclusion that these lower levels of chemicals must be the *cause* of the problem and that drugs could be administered to raise these levels to effectuate a cure. But this view makes little sense. Why? Because everything we think, feel, and do all day affects these chemicals in our brain. If you take a walk in the sunshine, your serotonin levels rise. If you eat a banana, your serotonin levels rise. Dopamine is involved in memory and learning processes as well as other brain functions. So many things activate chemicals in our brain throughout the day that nobody really knows what's going on at any given moment on a molecular or cellular level.

The problem is that it's too easy to label and stigmatize people with these conditions. The daytime television personality Dr. Oz had a panel of experts on one of his shows who all agreed that antidepressant drugs are harmful. Medical practitioners take these same antidepressant drugs that are prescribed to adults and, without any real long-term scientific testing, prescribe them for children as young as two and three years old. Do you actually believe your two-year-old is suffering from a disorder called Sluggish Cognitive Tempo and needs stimulant drugs? How young then are we willing to go? When babies cry too much or need to relieve themselves frequently will these become new disorders called Excessive Crying Disorder and Impulsive Need to Poop Syndrome? Think about the ramifications of giving a child whose brain is still developing a drug that's been tested only on adults and is known to be potentially harmful. Such children subsequently become dependent on these drugs and are labeled and stigmatized by teachers, peers, and the general culture. To further complicate matters, the children's brains are now abnormally changed by these powerful drugs—a situation which will make them susceptible to damage in numerous other ways in the future. Quite possibly, the children's mental ability to function normally has been permanently altered.

Let me give you an example. One problem in our society when we talk about antidepressant drugs concerns the mass-shooting incidents that seem to be occurring increasingly more often. Many of these gunmen were taking antidepressant or antipsychotic drugs. They were mostly young men who probably had significant emotional problems in the first place, but through incorrect treatment, their minds were altered by ingesting these toxic medications. Their brains were literally rewired in a dangerous way by these powerful drugs. Mental health professionals know this to be true—and yet our society allows the situation to continue unabated. It's yet another horrible example of why the prevailing ways we approach mental health care and addiction treatment in the United States as a one-size-fits-all, everything is a disease or chemical imbalance that can be treated with a medication approach, needs to be rethought. We are losing our humanity when we treat people in such a way.

My Italian grandmother wore a black dress every day for one year while grieving the death of my grandfather. The DSM-5 would have us believe that she was experiencing "Excessive Bereavement Syndrome" because she wasn't getting over her husband's death quickly enough and that perhaps antidepressants would help. Help with what? Being human? Sadness over the loss of a loved one doesn't make one diagnosable as sick or diseased. To feel heartache, loneliness, fear, or depression when a loved one dies, a divorce or romantic breakup occurs, or when one loses a job or financial security is completely human and subjectively experienced.

We must not lose the human connection of personal storytelling and allow overdiagnosing and overprescribing to simply be accepted as business as usual. For the people with severe mental problems drugs may be entirely necessary in order to keep them safe but this is a small percentage of people. However when drugs are prescribed simply as an expeditious way of avoiding a human connection, the benefits to humanity is dubious. All drugs affect the brain, and when we become dependent on them, it's no different than being dependent on alcohol, street drugs, or any addictive behavior, such as gambling, shopping, or overeating.

Because mental health and addiction treatment are so closely related there needs to be a shift in thinking. Today, we use rehabs as a place to treat co-occurring disorders, like a substance use disorder and depression. In doing so we maintain both problems because they are seen as lifelong ailments. If you are detoxifying someone from alcohol but maintain and encourage antidepressant use, you reinforce the language of powerlessness, hopelessness, and helplessness. The person learns to accept that they are psychologically and physically dependent for the rest of their lives. In the same way you don't need to be a drug addict to be arrested for possession or an alcoholic to get a DUI, you don't have to be mentally ill to be prescribed medication. I would maintain that for many people who have been given a dual diagnosis, perhaps they should seek to wean off their overdependence on prescription drugs with the help of a compassionate, nonjudgmental, and empathetic doctor, because without changing their subjectivity, addressing their underlying problems, and learning new ways to cope with their life challenges, they will always be discontented, frustrated, and unhappy with or without drugs.

8

CELEBRITY CULTURE AND ADDICTIVE BEHAVIOR

Many well-known people and the general public assume that having a "disease" must be the only explanation for why a rich and famous person would become self-destructive with addictive behaviors. Celebrities in American culture are rarely viewed as individuals with the same kinds of emotional problems, lack of coping skills, and unresolved early conflicts as the rest of us. Our media exploits bad behavior as entertainment if exhibited by rich, talented, and creative people. Tabloid news organizations remain in lockstep with the prevailing, disease-model approach to addiction via sensationalized news coverage. Rarely do you see "expert" guests on news shows that have a more progressive point of view based on the current knowledge and information available providing their input on a celebrity's misfortune.

> Megan is a twenty-year-old who works in a fashionable clothing store. She idolizes the troubled actress Lindsay Lohan. In fact, Megan has even seen her out in Los Angeles nightclubs. Megan likes to drink when she goes out and was stopped one night by police and charged with DUI. She knows the same event happened to Lindsay and has even heard her speak about her "disease" on talk shows and in magazine articles. Megan is now convinced she has the same disease and feels as though she shares something in common with a celebrity. She also figures that if Lindsay can't get it together, what chance does she have?

Dan is a forty-four-year-old attorney who's taking antidepressants for depression and attends AA meetings for his drinking problem. There he is told that he's powerlessness over his incurable "disease." Dan also sees a "celebrity addiction" doctor on TV programs talking about the dual-diagnosis of alcoholism and depression, and how both are incurable biological or genetic disorders. Dan subsequently becomes even more depressed and begins drinking again.

The power of the media and celebrity culture to influence public opinion is enormous. I would maintain that it contributes to maintaining these societal problems more than finding solutions to them. The media could choose to create the environments for healthy, intelligent discourse on these societal problems but like most individuals, we seek certainty. The need for certainty creates the façade of concern or caring for someone with high visibility. Think about it logically. We rarely see mental health problems including addictive behaviors as reality until something happens to a well-known person. Then we are flooded with ongoing news stories and TV panel discussions. This is a problem of perception. Celebrity tragedies create headline news and emotionally stir us. This makes people a captive audience to whatever messages and agendas are being disseminated.

For example, after Robert Williams's death the autopsy concluded that he took his own life and did not discover the presence of alcohol or illegal drugs. The results found "therapeutic" levels of prescription drugs. The news reported that he had Lewy body dementia, early stage Parkinson's disease, and a history of depression. He also had substance use problems years prior. As the public was shocked by this news the need for an explanation on how someone loved by millions could take his own life brought to center stage the problems of suicide, depression, substance use, mental disorders, and diseases. At the same time, we can learn from this sad and tragic ending to this exceptionally talented man's life that may help others. Here's what I think is important:

1. Nobody knows what is going on inside your head. This is what makes people unique. We all have subjective experiences. We can be happy on the outside and suffering on the inside. There is no expert for that.
2. Antidepressant drugs can increase depression and the thoughts of suicide.

3. He was in treatment. Yet, he continued to suffer. Everyone is different.
4. He had access to the "best care" in the world. So, what was that?

Yet, he came to a place where he believed he had no other options. A sad and lonely place that millions of nonfamous people reach every day without having access to help and with few if any people knowing or caring about them. This must change.

This is not a good time in our country to have a serious mental illness. Too many people with serious mental health problems are either homeless or in jail. This is disgraceful. Ten times as many people with serious mental health problems are in jail than in hospitals.

The next time you see a homeless person talking to himself/herself try to be more compassionate. This is someone's father, mother, brother, son, daughter, aunt, uncle, cousin, or friend. More importantly, they are human beings.

The influential psychological thinker Alfred Adler declared that "the early childhood feeling of inferiority, for which one aims to compensate, leads to the creation of a fictional final goal which subjectively seems to promise future security and success. The depth of the inferiority feeling usually determines the height of the goal which then becomes the "final cause" of behavioral efforts and patterns."[1] It's a view that's certainly relevant in our time, for many people in the entertainment industry believe that by gaining fame as an actor, musician, or singer, they'll surely lose their feelings of inferiority. If unsuccessful in achieving celebrity status, they usually continue to experience these feelings. Yet if they do attain such an exalted position in our culture, it still doesn't "fix" their problem—because it's deeply rooted in their personality, shaped years earlier during early childhood. In both cases, nothing will change as long as their self-talk and narrow framing of their subjectivity remains the same. The need for love, approval, and validation—manifested as an inferiority complex developed in their formative years—continues to control them. Thus, they can spend their whole lives searching for authenticity. Ironically, when celebrities attend AA or twelve-step-based programs, the identity they accept of being diseased and powerless actually reinforces their feelings of inferiority.

We live in a celebrity-driven culture. In the United States today the societal connection between celebrity culture and the treatment of substance use disorders and other addictive behaviors is never more obvious than when the media dictates the message by using these highly visible people to promote the establishment's agenda. Because there's a concerted effort to highlight the "disease model" of addiction in the media, few proponents of alternative treatment approaches are ever invited to appear on TV shows focusing on celebrity problems. Instead, "experts" are called upon to promote the medical or genetic viewpoint, which downplays social, cultural, and psychological factors. This emphasis is especially misguided because the entertainment industry attracts men and women with a particular personality type—craving attention and admiration. By promoting the idea that "addictions" are incurable, these programs give the public a misleading, dogmatic, and myopic point of view of a much more human and complex reality.

For example, many years ago Larry King moderated a celebrity panel on addiction on his CNN talk show. The panel included Dr. Drew Pinsky, actor Tom Arnold (former husband of Roseanne Barr), Mackenzie Phillips (former juvenile star and child of sixties rock star John Phillips), and Jane Velez-Mitchell (television host). The messages they were espousing? From Dr. Drew: addiction is a biological and genetic disease. From Tom Arnold: he mentioned AA's cofounder Bill Wilson and the wonderful free meetings available any night of the week. From Mackenzie Phillips: she'd recently been on Celebrity Rehab (Dr. Drew's reality show at the time) and had just written a book she was promoting. From Jane Velez-Mitchell: addiction is a spiritual disease and it needs a spiritual solution, namely, twelve-step meetings.

Not one of them simply suggested that they were experiencing some very difficult and challenging times in their lives and turned to substances to cope. They did not speak about their inability to regulate their choices. They were unraveling in their lives emotionally and needed an explanation, some sense of certainty. They did not discuss what prescription drugs they were dependent on or if they had researched any of the evidenced-based treatments that they would have easy access to if they chose to. Both Arnold and Phillips declared that their disease had rendered them almost completely nonfunctioning. But that's not the experience of most people with addictive behaviors who may have been watching this television show. Like most doctors, Dr. Drew subscribes to the disease model which explains his view on addiction.[2]

Velez-Mitchell admitted that her drinking began because she felt confused about her sexuality, which sounds more like an identity problem rather than a spiritual one. The entire show lacked open dialogue or exchange of new ideas regarding anything that was original. Of course I am sure their appearances helped some people. But we have to cast the net further. The appeal in front of millions of viewers should be to reach out to the diversity in people, their subjective realities, and the various degrees of severity of their problems. People may have similar problems but they are never identical because we all experience life in our own way.

Certainly, we see the power of many celebrities performing altruistic endeavors to better the lives of others. This is a great thing. Often self-indulgent and preoccupied by the immediacy of their own needs, these people thus gain a semblance of positive emotionality while benefiting others. However, when the topic is addiction treatment, I believe we would benefit as a society to actually hear a celebrity speak about how they overcame his/her drinking problem" or use a different language other than disease and powerless to affect and motivate change in others. This would be a great contribution to humanity as well. These creative and intelligent people—whose skills in other areas of their lives are highly developed—could thereby empower others by explaining how they solved their problems by using their mind's creativity to re-think their subjective life.

When we find ourselves fascinated by celebrities who appear on talk shows to discuss their "battle with their demons"—or by the sensationalized news coverage that follows the unfortunate death of a famous actor or pop star—we can acquire a false sense of similarity to these people. But the basic commonality of drug use we may have with a celebrity doesn't make us similar. If people struggling with any behavior looks to social media, the Internet, TV, or *People Magazine* as an informational source for certainty, they will be disappointed. From my coaching experience, those individuals who lacked authoritative (assertive, democratic, balanced) parenting while growing up are precisely those most vulnerable to the mass media's message about celebrity problems.

How so? Because in a variety of ways, celebrity culture undermines the authoritative parenting approach shown to have a beneficial psychological impact on development. It does so by promulgating the message that bad behavior is acceptable if done by talented, creative people. And those most easily influenced by our celebrity culture is our youth.

The 2013 death of Cory Monteith—the handsome star of the hit television series *Glee*—is illustrative of the way young people are given mixed messages about serious problems they are exposed to through celebrity media coverage. By all accounts, Monteith had received treatment for substance use both before and during his years on the show—and fulfilled all of his professional obligations. But after Monteith was found dead in a hotel room of a heroin and alcohol overdose, he was mourned through his character "Finn" in a highly rated episode that dealt with his fictional classmates and real-life cast-mates' pain and anguish in a blurring of the line between fiction and reality. However, there was one glaring omission. By ignoring the cause of "Finn's" death, *Glee* lost a crucial opportunity to educate its young fans about the dangers of drug use. That is, many people chastised the show's producers for failing to use their platform to help prevent more untimely deaths from substance abuse. Some even claimed that the producers downplayed the dangers of drug use by memorializing "Finn" without somehow working Monteith's years of substance abuse and his death from overdose into the episode's storyline.

For me, the message was indeed clear. *Glee*'s producers appealed to their loyal viewers coveted by advertisers and chose to sidestep the way the actor died by having the circumstances of his character's death remain a mystery. Perhaps they thought that having "Finn" die from a drug overdose would be too negative? Who knows, but regardless of this possibility, this was probably a missed opportunity to send a strong message to adolescents about the risks of drug use.[3] Last year, the award-winning actor Philip Seymour Hoffman died of a heroin overdose alone in his New York City office apartment. I'd like to know: when Hoffman was attending AA meetings, what information was given, or withheld from him? Did nobody tell him that using heroin and a variety of other drugs would intensify all his other drugs and could kill him? In a similar way that many people who attend AA continue to smoke in place of drinking, how does it make sense for someone like this talented actor to go years without drinking yet abuse a variety of other substances—and still attend AA meetings? Obviously, Hoffman was struggling with profound emotional difficulties that were not getting addressed. Why? It's *dopamine* that allowed him to memorize hundreds of pages of dialogue and show up on movie sets to spend long hours creating memorable characters. It logically follows that his brain functioned powerfully. Is it really possible he could not have been told—or did not know—that what he was doing was dangerous? You can't blame it on the disease. Disease is not a part-time gig. You have heart disease or you don't. You have diabetes or you don't.[4] Many people in show business struggle with emotional instability. They believe that they've little control over important aspects of their lives and the same trust and control issues that all people deal with are accentuated by someone whose personal identity is not necessarily congruent with their public identity. This contributes to the challenges they face with authentic friendships and romantic love. Because celebrities generally interact with other famous people, their social relationships make real intimacy more difficult and for many short-lived. Easy accessibility to others and the ease of establishing new relationships makes the interpersonal dimension appear simple for celebrities, but such people often share an unhealthy degree of neuroticism that usually results in temporary or transient relations. Authentic social support and emotional intimacy are difficult because many famous people fear being exploited by others—and therefore have few real friends in spite of millions of social media followers. They're simultaneously guarded and emotionally needy. That's a terrible condition to endure if those supporting them are more like sycophants rather than loving and caring.

Healthy self-esteem and self-worth is lacking among many celebrities who are self-destructive. This lack of self-esteem—and certainly their lack of self-compassion—coupled with the need for constant attention, fuels their ambition to achieve. The result? A masking of the person's true self, which is often quite fragile. Many high profile men and women present a false image to the public (certainly with the ample help of their managers and publicists). Their sense of perceived control over their lives is tentative and their addictive behaviors undermine even this limited sense of control. In many cases, their addictive behaviors are an attempt to escape from the ever-gnawing reminder that their success (and by extension their personal value) is relevant only to the degree to which they're admired by the public and enhance the profits of their employers.

In my coaching work, I've likewise found that many socially recognized and financially successful people suffer from chronic problems of anxiety, depression, and low self-esteem. People are always amazed when they discover that someone whom they assume has a wonderful, glamorous life actually experiences chronic distress. They wonder how someone who is rich and famous—for example, a celebrated actor, entertainer, or athlete—could be so successful professionally and can be self-sabotaging. The influence of celebrity culture—especially on younger people—and its alignment with AA and twelve-step programs gives a mixed message to the public. In a very real sense, celebrities with very real human problems are "foot soldiers" for the treatment industry when they behave badly. The public knows the cycle all too well. The celebrity who behaves badly first apologizes, then blames the action on having a disease, enters and leaves a posh rehab center to the accompaniment of news photos—and then typically begins the process anew after a few years, or sometimes after only a few months or weeks.

For example, Charlie Sheen has always been well liked by the public. He was among the highest paid stars on TV and has made a lot of money for networks and producers. His hard-partying, womanizing character when he appeared on the hit television show *Two and a Half Men* is largely based on himself—so it's difficult to separate fiction from reality. This situation was part of the show's appeal. Sheen has admittedly tried the conventional AA and twelve-step treatment approach for his addictive behaviors over the years with little success. But for the most part his erratic behavior, as long as it didn't interfere with his professional obligations, was generally overlooked. When Sheen crossed the line in 2011—a situation which led to his much publicized, bitter parting with CBS and the *Two and a Half Men* producers—everyone who'd looked the other way in the past quickly pointed to his disease to explain his personal unraveling.

But for those who subscribe to the disease model of addiction—suggesting that Sheen's brain had become disordered and therefore he lacked control over his behavior—I must point out that his disease appeared to be working only part time. After all, it didn't seem to affect his ability to handle the myriad pressures of headlining a hit TV series for the many years leading up to his meltdown. By all accounts, he'd been the consummate professional on the set of his show—all the while overindulging in alcohol and drugs in his off-time.[5]

Of course, I'm not defending Mr. Sheen's behavior in any way. I'm simply pointing out that I'm not aware of anyone who has a disease that can be turned on and off easily. However, as a rationalization for bad behavior, reducing everything to biology is convenient for those who benefit. Virtually all people from diverse walks of life who overindulge in addictive behaviors share a common profile: They require immediate gratification as a way to relieve emotional distress. Most people with ongoing addictive behaviors have never addressed their underlying problems, which generally revolve around poor coping skills, low self-esteem, early developmental difficulties, trauma, fear, or an identity crisis. These unresolved problems usually manifest as unhappiness, immaturity, inappropriateness, or disrespect for themselves and others—belying a selfish, self-indulgent, and narcissistic worldview. This shapes their subjective experience.

This is all learned behavior, reinforced by many influences. But it's still behavior based upon free will and choice. Medicalizing human experiences is just a construct. Yes, many of these problematic behaviors are detrimental to the individual and to society—but that doesn't make it a literal disease. Here again, the reductionist point of view would have suggested Charlie Sheen has the dual diagnosis of a substance use disorder and a mental disorder. But what purpose do those labels actually serve?

The language of addiction needs to be changed and redefined. Its current use of circular reasoning is misleading especially for the majority of people whose problematic behaviors are not detrimental to themselves or others. For example, if you enter the rehab system and admit to being an alcoholic, you have a disease. If you don't admit to being an alcoholic, you are still viewed as having a disease—but now you're considered to be in denial. The implication is that the denial is a symptom of the disease. Keep in mind: an abused thirteen-year-old girl who runs away from home, begins using drugs as a form of emotional relief, and winds up in a residential treatment center will be told she too has a disease. A gay teenager struggling with his sexuality who turns to drinking to numb his emotional pain will be told he has a disease. A woman who drinks only on rare occasions but becomes intoxicated at a family gathering and is stopped for a DUI will be told she has a disease. The disease label is an arbitrary term used to deal with bad behavior regardless of the causes that created the behavior. For the lack of creativity, the default explanation for problematic behavior suffered by many people having human experiences is simply to state with certainty that it is a literal disease.

Does Lindsay Lohan have a disease? Many young women who are the same age as when she was when she began having problems are behaving in the same reckless way. But since she's well known, she's made into a public spectacle partly because of her ability to generate tabloid stories, proffer huge fees to attorneys and rehab facilities, and pay fines to the courts. Keep in mind, the NIAAA states that most people who experience substance abuse problems have an episodic experience lasting about four years, with the onset occurring between the late teens and early to mid-twenties. Ms. Lohan at the time may have just been part of the normal majority of college-age people who overindulge between the ages of eighteen and twenty-five and then moderate their behavior thereafter. Instead of being given the opportunity to possibly grow out of this wild and irresponsible stage, she's labeled with a brain disease that she'll now need to deal with for the rest of her life.[6] This trend of labeling extreme behavior immediately as a mental illness is unnerving for all college-age young adults who binge drink on occasion. But according to more recent research, those who overindulged during these years can now rest easy—it didn't harm their brain cells.

The *New York Times* reported that research at the State University of New York at Buffalo by Dr. Roberta J. Pentney found that "alcohol disrupts brain function in adults by damaging message-carrying dendrites on neurons in the cerebellum, a structure involved in learning and motor coordination. This reduces communication between neurons, alters their structure, and causes some of the impairment associated with intoxication. It does not kill off entire cells, however."[7]

I'm not defending Lindsay Lohan's inappropriate behavior, I'm simply pointing out that it's not necessarily indicative of a physical disease or a mental illness. This is why labeling people can be harmful. You cannot assess and diagnose everyone as though they were on an assembly line. If you believe that addiction is a biological disease and that the brain is disordered, then how can you expect a person with a disordered brain to consciously choose to stop their behavior or else be considered a failure? This would be akin to telling cancer patients who don't go into remission that they are responsible for the failure of the treatment. If you label Lindsay Lohan's problems as biological and that she's powerless, then why would you send her to jail for being incapable of controlling herself? In essence, she's being asked to take responsibility for her behavior but she's told that her problems are indicative of a disease whose symptoms include the inability to control one's behavior. Does this viewpoint make sense?

The general public is unaware that celebrities are treated differently in a myriad of ways. It's hypocritical to suggest that people are looking out for a celebrity's best interests when nightclubs offer to pay a celebrity to show up and party at their establishment, and treatment centers offer to waive their fees when a celebrity checks into their rehab facility. Celebrities enter treatment in a vastly different way than the average person. They typically go to beautiful locations like Malibu and spend their days in very comfortable surroundings. Their daily routine might include therapy sessions complemented by optional activities like swimming, yoga, tennis, access to a gym, horseback riding, and great meals. Of course the costs of these luxuries (treatment) are quite substantial.

Such interventions are essentially mini get-a-ways and a good public-relations move in many instances. Several rehab facilities in Malibu, California, can cost more than $50,000 a month.

Celebrities themselves are even getting into the residential recovery business. The actor Matthew Perry recently opened Perry House—a seven-bed, AA and twelve-step approach sober-living men's facility in his former beach house, an ultramodern glass building that offers ocean views, a surround sound theater, and a lap pool with a flat-screen TV overhead.[8] This and other group homes like it, in which residents live under supervision without receiving treatment, are proliferating by all accounts. But treatment centers and sober-living houses have been criticized for inflating their success rates. According to John Kelly, director of the Addiction Recovery Management Service at Massachusetts General Hospital and an associate professor of psychiatry at Harvard Medical School, "There aren't hard figures, but on average probably only a third of residential program inpatients are still sober one year after intervention."[9]

The standard being used to measure treatment success is simply being abstinent. I know this is the easiest way to quantify information. It's simple. Yes, I am still drinking or, no, I am not. But, I disagree. I want to know how and if these people have learned new coping skills. I want to know if they are experiencing more positive well-being. How are they functioning in other areas of their life? Are they smoking a pack of cigarettes a day or overeating? Are they in healthy relationships? Are they taking antidepressant drugs every day? What happens after they leave rehab? What happens when they're not being monitored twenty-four/seven and are triggered by an environmental stressor? I want to know how has their subjective experiences changed. I want to know how their thinking, feeling, and beliefs have evolved.

It's impossible to discuss the impact of celebrity culture on the general public without touching on narcissism. For decades, mental health theorists have associated entertainment stars with the narcissistic personality. Such writings have come mainly from two psychoanalytic thinkers: Heinz Kohut and Otto Kernberg. Both based their influential formulations on the seminal work of Sigmund Freud, who viewed narcissism as self-love coupled with fragile self-esteem, fear of failure, and other factors. According to the last DSM, narcissism is a personality disorder marked by an exaggerated sense of self-importance and uniqueness, an unreasonable sense of entitlement and exploitative tendencies toward others. Many mental health professionals today believe that narcissism is increasing, especially among our youth. This notion received dramatic empirical support in a recent cross-temporal study showing that almost two-thirds of recent college graduates register above the average narcissism score.

But what makes some of us narcissistic? How and when does it happen? Most children show narcissistic features until about age seven or eight before maturing into a more realistic view of themselves. Based on recent findings, the exceptions appear to be those raised by either chronically inattentive or overly admiring parents. Most experts agree that narcissistic individuals learn early in life to put themselves on a pedestal either to live up to parental expectations or to compensate for a lack of parental warmth. Narcissistic traits imprint during childhood development and result in a personality that seeks constant attention, adoration, love, approval, and validation—having insufficiently completed these early stages.

There is a link between narcissism, substance use disorder, and celebrity culture. Celebrities score significantly higher on the scale of narcissism than the general population, despite the fact that years of experience in the entertainment industry were not associated with higher levels of narcissism. This finding suggests that those entering the field were already higher than the norm. Those with narcissistic personality traits feel they deserve lavish praise and special treatment, crave being the center of attention, and "know" they are remarkable and secretly envied by others. Many young people today take their cues from celebrity culture and pursue their need for attention and relevancy on social media sites like Facebook, Instagram, Twitter, and YouTube.

Lack of personal responsibility and an aversion to delayed gratification are part of addictive behaviors for both the famous as well as many nonfamous people. More than ever, it seems that men and women today are not being reinforced to behave in a consistently mature, appropriate, and respectful manner. The harmful consequences of this trend are all around us. We are what we think. It's easier for some to accept they have a disease because the alternative is self-reflection, self-discovery, hard work, and real desire and motivation to change. That's something many people are unwilling to do—and therefore, like their addictive behavior itself, their struggles continue. Their need for quick fixes and easy explanations continue to define them, mostly to their detriment.

One thing I have learned from teaching minority students from low socioeconomic backgrounds, many of whom struggle with addictive behaviors, mental challenges, and are on probation or parole for drug-related violations is that they obviously can't afford $50,000 a month for treatment. Their treatment looks much different. But it is still predicated on deficit-based language. At the same time I have also come to realize that both groups, the rich and poor and the famous and the nonfamous, share something in common. They all are having unhappy subjective experiences. They all have a narrow view of their perceived and practical realities. They all are human beings first and all trying to cope with their life challenges. They all are unique individuals in search of love, approval, validation, joy, happiness, and life satisfaction. No amount of money can change someone's subjective experience: the experience of living with your own thoughts, emotions, and realities.

9

PARENTING INFLUENCE ON CHILDREN

Children learn to cope with life problems by watching their parents. Research shows that parents who are authoritarian (obedience-oriented or punitive) or permissive (lax or indulgent) run the risk of causing their children to develop psychological difficulties that often lead to problematic behaviors. Studies reveal that the authoritative (assertive, democratic, and balanced) parenting style supports healthier psychological development in children. While we like to make the connection of offspring difficulties with substances as running in families—for example, suggesting that alcoholism/drug addiction has a genetic component—the same conclusion can be made that these families lack positive role modeling and the fostering of healthy coping skills in successive generations. As the saying goes, *the apple doesn't fall far from the tree.*

Our brains and our personalities develop by early childhood learning experiences. Our parents and/or primary caregivers are our first role models from which we learn how to cope with life challenges and difficult circumstances. We learn by observation, imitation, and modeling. If our parents are emotionally unstable and abuse drugs or alcohol in front of us when we are children, the experience gets "downloaded" and unconsciously becomes familiar to us. Because we also need love, approval, and validation from our parents, we learn to accept as "normal" the drama and chaos that we might be exposed to and that is associated with these behaviors.

We are all familiar with the term ADHD (Attention Deficit Hyper-activity Disorder) and drugs like Ritalin and Adderall are given to millions of kids between the ages of four and seventeen. No matter how you feel about giving children drugs for behavioral problems, it's important to see the bigger picture.

Those who argue for giving children drugs indicate that when they work, they really work and the most severe child is suddenly able to focus and pay attention and get along with his family, friends, and classmates much better. That sounds good and it is good, right?

At the same time, there are ethical problems. There is no research that exists on the long-term impact of such drugs on the future development of a child in terms of their brain and personality development. All drugs have a variety of effects. Also, keep in mind, no medical test actually determines if a child has ADHD. It is a subjective diagnosis often made by doctors based solely on a set of signs and symptoms dealing with observing the child's behavior. Many children outgrow these same symptoms without being labeled as having ADHD or taking drugs.

As I mentioned previously, there now comes new information from the Centers for Disease Control and Prevention (CDC) that estimates more than ten thousand U.S. toddlers, aged two to three, are being given stimulant drugs for behaviors that are observed to be like ADHD called Sluggish Cognitive Tempo.[1] Here's my concern. Will the normal development stage known as the "terrible twos" now be considered a mental illness? Would you give a child a drug so they do not go through this developmental period? Then what? Do doctors start to observe babies and decide that their behavior is not normal either? We worry about drugs like nicotine and marijuana and refer to them as "gateway" drugs. What about the effects of chemicals on a child's developing brain? If it's thought of as "medicine" to treat a mental disorder it's considered neuroprotective. But if it's a drug that is used to socially bond with a peer group its dangerous.

> Gabriela is a thirteen-year-old girl whose parents fight all the time. There's constant tension in her home. Her father copes by drinking heavily and her mother is morbidly obese from binge eating. Gabriela is overweight and recently began drinking and hanging out with other troubled adolescents at her junior high school. She posts suggestive, age-inappropriate photos of herself under a fictitious name

on social media sites. Gabriela is also sexually active with a much older boy and neither of them uses any form of birth control.

Brad is an eighteen-year-old college freshman on his own for the first time. His parents were very controlling and wouldn't even let him try a beer at home under their supervision. They're extremely religious and believe alcohol is evil. Having no previous experience with alcohol and feeling peer pressure to fit in on campus, Brad began drinking heavily. The effects were so emotionally liberating that he quickly became addicted. His parents' rigid beliefs about social drinking made this behavior all the more attractive to him on an unconscious level as a way to rebel and gain independence from them.

Relationships within the family unit set the stage for adolescent coping mechanisms, whether positive or negative. Research suggests that problematic interaction with parents and peers often leads to an increase in addictive behaviors in teenagers. Parental control and rejection have been shown to catalyze the development of depression and anxiety in the youth population. Parents must become aware of their children's changing thoughts and beliefs to address their emotional functioning in a timely manner—and thereby help eliminate the development of substance or behavioral problems. The diagnoses of anxiety disorders and depression are often just labels given by physicians looking for a quick fix and can cause impressionable adolescents to believe that they've no possibility to feel better. Why are the rates of addiction and mental health problems surging among children and teens today? What are we missing? These are questions every parent should ponder.

In my years of coaching practice, I've found that the issues at hand are never what they seem. For example, weight problems and obesity aren't really about food, but primarily about self-esteem and other underlying problems. Addictive behaviors are not about the substance or actual behavior, but rather the reasons for needing a relationship with them. Problems now confronting adolescents seem more challenging than ever. Depression and anxiety are on the rise, and more and more teens are struggling. Studies of youthful depression and anxiety consistently show the effects of the family environment play a major role in either optimizing or constricting adolescent functioning. Parents must examine their children's self-perceptions and beliefs, life stressors, problem-solving skills, and school and social life. For example, peer victimization and bullying are becoming more prominent than ever before. The media presents numerous cases of children as young as age twelve ending their lives because of victimization—which can occur in many forms, including physical, emotional, social media bullying, and threatening text messages.

Why are some adolescents able to see themselves through the lens of emotional positivity and possess an ability to deal effectively with life's stressors, compared to those who cannot? What determines who has high or low self-esteem? How do environmental factors affect outcomes? Why does mattering to their peers have such an influential effect on adolescents in relation to depression and anxiety? Are we missing the boat with regard to early identification and therefore to prevention as well?

Kids today are learning to expect immediate gratification, rather than anticipate effort in many areas of their lives including physical appearance, social relationships, and academic and athletic achievement. What does this have to do with addictive behaviors? Simply this: addiction is about filling a void. If you're superficial, you're in need of substance. If you're in need of substance, you look for immediate gratification to satisfy your own self-interests. These qualities in a person suggest a conflict in understanding one's values, life direction, and what's required to attain one's desires and goals. This entire process produces anxiety, stress, and depression. Lacking the skill sets necessary to manage such emotional states, teens, or younger seek quick fixes with drugs, alcohol, social media, texting, and other common age behaviors. Our educational system doesn't teach life skills and doesn't prepare children to think critically, practically, and resourcefully.

Observational learning, or social learning, occurs when children determine how to behave in differing circumstances and deal with common problems by observing their parents' behavior. Children whose parents exhibit hostility toward each other, or who are abused or neglected, or who relocate frequently, all tend to suffer from lower self-esteem. They're also attracted to other emotionally distant and toxic people because such behaviors are familiar. If your parents argued all the time, had physical altercations with each other, or were chronically stressed about bills, work, and other everyday situations—these were your first learning experiences in developing coping strategies of your own.

So what happened? You learned to deal with stress and anxiety in your adult life and relationships in the same way as your parents did—that is, immaturely, inappropriately, and disrespectfully. When you learn to behave in this way, you'll then use these poor coping strategies to attempt releasing your own inner tension and anxiety. If you daily witness bad behavior, you learn to regard it as *normal*. If those around you abused alcohol and drugs to cope with distress in their lives, you learned that this behavior was normal, too.

According to developmental theories, our personality is formed by around age seven and the seeds for our future emotional functioning are thereby planted. This concept suggests that if we think of our brain as a computer, then all our software has been downloaded by the age of seven. This is when our self-esteem and self-image come together. In particular, narcissism will take root if the mother doesn't give her child enough attention—for this situation causes the child to seek approval and validation from others. Such children grow into adults who'll hold the objects of their desire on a pedestal (known clinically as idealization) or put them down with judgments and criticism when they fear rejection or abandonment (known clinically as devaluation). Although this process is not a sole explanation for addictive behavior, it may interact with other causes and increase its likelihood.

For example, if children grow up in families that allow frequent irrational outbursts of anger, then observational learning can play a role in their tendency toward chronic anger. The evidence is strong that parents lacking the authoritative style are more likely to foster substance abuse as well as narcissism in their offspring. Indeed some theorists have argued that basically *all addictions are problems of narcissism*. This is a view that has merit.

Psychologists, therapists, and healthcare providers continually come back to the same basic question: "Why do adolescents engage in behaviors they know are detrimental to their physical and mental health?" The Adverse Childhood Experiences (ACE) series of studies conducted by the CDC show direct correlations between childhood exposure to abuse or neglect and higher rates in adulthood of chronic health problems, high-risk addictive behaviors, and shortened lifespan.[2] The 2009 publication, "Hidden Costs in Healthcare: The Economic Impact of Violence and Abuse" states that "studies show child abuse is a major life stressor that has consequences involving the mental health of the future adult including increased risk factors for the development of substance abuse related problems and a significantly higher rate of anxiety and depression."[3]

Since such information is available to healthcare professionals, one would think that an emphasis on a holistic approach to caring for children in the areas of physical, behavioral, and mental health would be the norm. Unfortunately, the exact opposite is true. For example, a recent study by Medco Health Solutions found that nearly 25 percent of American children are regularly taking pharmaceutical drugs originally intended for adults only. These powerful drugs carry with them unknown side effects for long-term use in children. Dr. Daniel Benjamin, a professor of pediatrics at Duke University, admitted in a 2010 *Wall Street Journal* report that prescribing psychiatric medications for children is a serious problem and stated, "We know that doctors are making errors in dosing and safety."[4]

Psychiatric drugs given to children have been documented by drug regulatory agencies to have severe and life-threatening side effects. Millions of children have been diagnosed with ADHD, Bipolar Disorder, Obsessive Compulsive Disorder, and Social Anxiety Disorder—none of which is confirmed by science as a physical malfunction (disease). Instead, parents are simply told their child is mentally ill and more often than not, advised to place them on pharmaceutical drugs which the U.S. Drug Enforcement Administration (DEA) categorizes in the same class as cocaine, morphine, and opium.[5] Children are simply not being provided with nondrug solutions for problems involving attention, mood, or behavior.

Harvard psychologist Jerome Kagan is among the world's leading experts on child development. In an interview for the German weekly magazine *Der Spiegel*, he offered a scathing critique of the mental health establishment and pharmaceutical companies, accusing them of incorrectly classifying millions as mentally ill out of self-interest and greed.[6] Likewise, in a February 2012 article in *Der Spiegel*, the American psychiatrist Leon Eisenberg, who was the "scientific father of ADHD," said in his last interview before his death that "ADHD is a prime example of a fictitious disease." The use of ADHD medications in Germany between 1993 and 2011 rose from 34 kg to a record of no less than 1,760 kg which is a fifty-one-fold increase in sales in only eighteen years! In the United States every tenth boy among ten year olds already swallows an ADHD medication on a daily basis.[7] Even the National Institute of Health (NIH) issued a statement admitting, "We do not have an independent, valid test for ADHD, and there is no data to indicate that ADHD is due to a brain malfunction."[8]

A study published in the peer-reviewed *Journal of Child and Adolescent Psychopharmacology* (JCAP) found that the use of stimulant medications to treat ADHD in children and adolescents has increased significantly over the past several years for children as young as three. The report stated that U.S. sales of ADHD drugs more than doubled between 2007 and 2012, from $4 billion to $9 billion.[9] All this drugging of children rests on one fraudulent premise: that mental disorders are biological "diseases," therefore justifying the administration of pharmaceutical drugs. The falsity of this premise is easily established by noting that not one medical or scientific test can prove that a child has a mental disorder. The exception, of course, is that some children diagnosed with ADHD or other learning or behavioral disorders have been damaged by lead poisoning or by maternal drug or alcohol usage during pregnancy—and such damage can be identified by medical tests.

Clearly, I'm not asserting that many children may not have emotional or behavioral problems. Rather, I'm saying that without evidence of a disease—a physical disease—many children are simply being drugged to change their behavior. Even given "safely" in therapeutic doses, a child is learning to associate his/her own vulnerability with a dependency mind-set. Psychiatrists know this; their own literature admits as much, but they mostly like to keep quiet about these facts. The first thing parents should know if their teen or preteen is experimenting with drugs, alcohol, or any other addictive substance or behavior is that since there are no medical tests to prove their child is diseased or mentally ill—and that any diagnosis of a mental disorder is based solely on subjective criteria so they should ask to see the relevant proof.

Parents are rarely given the documented facts about the psychoactive drugs prescribed for their children, yet it's their right to have full information. If drugs are recommended for your child, then print out the summaries of drug warnings and studies on whatever type of drug is being recommended and provide them to the physician making the recommendation. Ask the doctor if he is aware of the studies and warnings on the risks of these drugs—because believe it or not, many doctors get their information on drug safety solely from pharmaceutical sales reps. In my view, it's unethical to prescribe antidepressant or anti-anxiety drugs to children except in the most extreme cases, when all other options for treatment have already been tried.

We must understand that antidepressants and other drugs like Ritalin are really the "gateway" drugs because they teach the young new consumer to develop a dependency mindset. In both the mass media and our educational system, it's a common topic that we're worried about our kids smoking cigarettes, using marijuana and consuming alcohol because such habits will lead them to the "harder" drugs like heroin, cocaine, and methamphetamine. But that's not really the whole story. The truth is we're introducing the drugs to children at younger and younger ages, accepting it as "normal" at a time when their brains are still developing—and the gateway drugs are the antidepressants, stimulants, and antipsychotic drugs.

Let's examine the entire idea of addictive behavior from the vantage point of the educational system. We don't teach coping skills, social skills, and critical thinking in American public schools. We teach and promulgate standardization: the practice of making all educators teach the same information. We shovel the information to students, then students take standardized tests to regurgitate the information we've told them to memorize. That is increasingly the foundation for our educational system. There's very little creativity, independent thinking, or diversity of learning experiences. In some school districts, students are actually prevented from learning anything new that may challenge the authority that's in place.

Curriculums must be preapproved by various authorities prior to implementation, and this process generally moves at a glacial pace. This situation hinders growth, change, and the adopting of new discoveries for students at all levels. As a community college instructor, I'm assigned a specific book by administrators each semester that I'm expected to follow in my lesson plans and homework assignments. I find that I'm always having to expand on this material with new, up-to-date findings to give my students the latest information on the topics we discuss in class. Unless I take the time to seek out the latest findings on the subject we're covering, I'd be teaching concepts that are often outdated.

The American public education system is set up to train students through operant conditioning by taking thinking out of the space between stimulus and response, and filling it with a controlling agenda. The space between stimulus and response gives us choice, freedom, liberty, and all the things that a child needs to grow into a healthy, autonomous adult capable of critical thinking. It's where we exercise our ability to reason. As conscious human beings, we must use reason to survive, we must know what knowledge looks like to dismiss the arbitrary and to spot misinformation and deception. The controllers don't want people to accomplish this, because then their agenda to direct the conversation would be exposed.

Our educational system trains children through operant conditioning in much the same way as scientists train pigeons to appear as if they're reading by pecking at the "right" words to receive food rewards. When they "diagnose" a child with ADHD, what they're really saying is that if a kid doesn't want to pay attention to things he finds boring, then he has ADHD and needs to be medicated. But why as a parent would you automatically accept that your child has a disease? Perhaps he can focus and pay attention to things that are really interesting, but prefers to ignore boring things. Maybe that's a good thing. If you accept the idea that your child has a disease without question, you give up your own power and voice. That's not a positive role model.

Overall, the goal of the educational system in America is not to educate children but to indoctrinate them. The addiction treatment industry functions in much the same way. We're culturally indoctrinated to believe that addiction is a disease. This is a notion that's been socially constructed by the institutions of government, big business, and religion. Addiction as a disease is not based on any science per se but rather on the necessity to create a standardized system. So, whether it's our political leaders, judicial system, educational system, or the addiction treatment industry, everybody uses the same language. Treatment therefore becomes cost-effective. Those who wield power in the addiction treatment industry have no incentive to learn evidence-based approaches of helping patients because that would mean they'd have to treat each individual as unique, and that would take more time and money. They would also have to learn new things.

Think of the "addiction industry" as a curriculum that subscribes to the disease model, a situation that makes it easy for clinicians to treat all individuals in the same way—not unlike a factory's assembly line. Consider the prevailing treatments we have for addictive behaviors. You essentially have a drug counselor you'll meet at a treatment center, who may not have any formal education in medicine or psychology, and who'll tell you that all addictive behaviors are diseases. You have AA and twelve-step programs which tell people that they have an incurable disease and are powerless to overcome it. You have psychiatrists who can bill insurance companies for a patient visit after seeing a person for a few minutes and writing a prescription. It's simple, easy, and highly profitable.

American colleges and universities are filled with the young and naive, feeling pressure to perform academically to justify the debt load of an education that may provide meager security in a shrinking job market. What better place for drug companies to hunt for uninformed new customers? Sending your child to college can now earn him a degree as well as a psychiatric disorder diagnosis. On-campus counseling services encourage students to visit psychiatrists' offices for quick fix drug solutions to their mostly age-appropriate concerns. The JED Foundation networks with colleges to set up comprehensive systems for mental health services. It boasts two past presidents of the APA on its board. JED's medical director, Dr. Victor Schwartz, writes: "In the past year, 21.2% of college students received a psychiatric diagnosis or were treated for mental health issues such as depression or eating disorders, and an estimated 6.6% of students reported having serious thoughts of suicide."[10]

One out of five college students now has a mental disorder? Can this possibly be true? American culture has been indoctrinated to believe that anyone who has problems related to drinking or drugs is necessarily a chronic and progressively disordered person who has no choice but to accept that they have a disease from which recovery is only possible through lifelong efforts. This is simply not true. If it were, the majority of college students and young adults who frequent fraternities, bars, and nightclubs and party to excess would be considered to have serious alcohol and drug problems. On the contrary, research shows that binge drinking behavior ceases for the majority of young adults once they leave college. It's been this way for generations. Chances are if you're over the age of thirty-five, you can recall many moments from your college days when—if viewed by today's standard of criteria for diagnosis—you too would have been told you had a mental disorder and prescribed a toxic drug.

In his landmark book, *Toxic Psychiatry*, Dr. Peter Breggin commented: "Roberta was a college student getting good grades, mostly A's, when she first became depressed and sought psychiatric help at the recommendation of her university health service. She was eighteen at the time, bright and well-motivated, and a very good candidate for psychotherapy. She was going through a sophomore-year identity crisis about dating men, succeeding in school, and planning a future. She could have thrived with a sensitive therapist who had an awareness of women's issues. Instead of moral support and insight her doctor gave her Haldol, an antipsychotic drug. Over the next four years, six different physicians watched her deteriorate neurologically without warning her or her family about the possibility that she might be suffering from tardive dyskinesia [motor brain damage] even when she was overtly twitching in her arms and legs. Instead they switched her from one antipsychotic drug to another. Eventually a rehabilitation therapist became concerned enough to send her to a general physician, who made the diagnosis of medical drug damage but by then she was permanently disabled, with a loss of 30 percent of her IQ."[11]

The general physician's medical evaluation described her condition as follows: "Roberta is a grossly disfigured and severely disabled human being who can no longer control her body. She suffers from extreme writhing movements and spasms involving nearly her entire body. She has difficulty standing, sitting, or lying down, and the difficulties worsen as she attempts to carry out voluntary actions. She could hold a cup to her lip only with great difficulty. Even her respiratory movements are seriously afflicted so that her speech comes out in grunts and gasps amid spasms of her respiratory muscles. . . . Roberta may improve somewhat after several months off the anti-psychotic drugs, but she will never again have anything remotely resembling a normal life."[12]

Several years ago, two state judges were arrested for accepting bribes from a private residential treatment center for juvenile offenders. To receive cash payments, the judges agreed to deliver harsh verdicts for minor infractions by falsely labeling kids as serious offenders. In many cases, they destroyed the lives of young people who were merely struggling with the challenges of growing up and had made mistakes no more serious than the average traffic violation. The "kids for cash" scandal unfolded in 2008 over judicial kickbacks at the Luzerne County Court of Common Pleas in Wilkes-Barre, Pennsylvania.

President Judge Mark Ciavarella and Senior Judge Michael Conahan were accused of accepting money from the builder of two private for-profit juvenile facilities. Bribes were paid to them in return for imposing harsh sentences on juveniles brought before their courts to increase the number of inmates in the detention centers. Judge Ciavarella sentenced children to extended stays in juvenile detention for offenses as minimal as mocking a principal on Myspace, trespassing in a vacant building, or shoplifting a DVD from Walmart.

In February 2011 a federal jury convicted Ciavarella of crimes in which prosecutors said the former judge used children "as pawns to enrich himself" with illegal payments of nearly $1 million. He was sentenced to twenty-eight years in federal prison. In September 2011 Judge Conahan was sentenced to seventeen years in federal prison for receiving bribes to needlessly incarcerate children for minor nonviolent infractions.[13] In *Help at Any Cost: How the Troubled- Teen Industry Cons Parents and Hurts Kids*, which is the first book-length exposé of the "tough love" business and how it fails to provide any positive coping skills for adolescents, Maia Szalavitz asks, "Where did this idea come from, the idea that kids need to be broken through public humiliation and emotional and physical attacks in order to be 'cured' of drug problems? Where did we get the idea that hurting kids will help them?"[14]

Psychologist Abraham Maslow suggested that teenagers turn to drugs and alcohol as ways of coping with stress in their lives, and that many are simply depressed and bored. Changing the face of depression and anxiety in adolescents by supporting them to build a positive self-concept that supports growth and encourages the improvement in the quality of thinking is imperative for us as a culture. An October 2011 report in *National Geographic Magazine* noted that the United States spends about one billion dollars per year on programs to counsel adolescents on the dangers of violence, gangs, suicide, sex, substance abuse, and other potential pitfalls, and that few of them work. One of the main reasons cited for this lack of positive outcomes is a failure to understand what scientists call the "Teenage Brain." According to Douglas Fields, a NIH neuroscientist, "studies show that the development of the frontal areas of the brain and the fatty myelin insulation (the brain's white matter) isn't fully completed for most people until their late teens or early twenties, therefore labeling teens and prescribing psychoactive drugs for risky behavior that is quite normal for their age group can have serious long term consequences for individuals and society as a whole."[15]

We must be sure that the help we're offering teens with substance abuse problems is actually working. Studies suggest that labeling their experimental drug and alcohol use as being in some way a chronic disease will ultimately have negative consequences by leading them to accept labels of being sick and disordered. California's Drug, Alcohol, and Tobacco Education (DATE) programs, which are nearly identical to national programs, have been shown to be largely ineffective in influencing students' decisions regarding drug use and may have negative effects according to a study published in the *Education Evaluation and Policy Analysis*, a national research journal.

In the study, 43 percent of California students surveyed said the state's drug education programs, such as Drug Abuse Resistance Education (DARE) and Red Ribbon Week, had no effect on their decisions to use drugs.[16] Joel H. Brown, PhD, director of Educational Research Consultants in Berkeley, California, stated, "Perhaps even the most advanced drug education programs believed to be effective in the United States were not." Brown reported that although the public believes there to be variety in drug education programs, there's actually only a narrow range of programs because federal law mandates that all drug education be zero-tolerance or abstinence-based. The "no substance use" message contributes to drug education program failure. Brown added further, "Youth believe the information they receive is inaccurate and misleading because the programs equate substance use with abuse and do not reflect the students' actual observations and experiences." Based on the research, Brown asserted that the programs are "harmful and have an effect counter to what is intended because students who believe the programs are dishonest may do the opposite of what they're being told."[17]

Consider the implications of such labeling for children and teenagers. If you take a thirteen-year-old boy who gets into trouble for drinking or taking drugs and is sent to a teen rehab facility, he's usually treated in the AA or twelve-step approach or other confrontational method. He's told that he has a disease, is powerless, and will have to go to meetings and be abstinent for the rest of his life. How reasonable is that? How effective do you think that's going to be? Children and teenagers develop a normal curiosity about alcohol, drugs, and sex.

What is going to occur when you tell them they can't do something? What is created when they're labeled early on in life after an episode of experimentation that went too far? We already know with sex education that when teens are told that abstinence before marriage is the only way to prevent teen pregnancy, there's an increase in other sexual activities.

If your child experiments with drugs or alcohol, or has another addictive behavior that you're worried about, get all the facts and explore an evidence-based approach to dealing with the problem whenever possible. Get a second, third, and fourth opinion on all major health decisions, conduct research on the Internet, ask questions, and become a critical thinker. Don't let your child take a psychoactive medication unless it's absolutely necessary. Realize your child's brain is developing and teach coping skills as early as you can. Don't let society or the medical establishment label and stigmatize your children in a way that may be damaging for the rest of their lives. Remember, some research shows that these medications are often the cause of "brain abnormalities" in children and may cause irreversible damage. There are many reasons why young people feel pain, experience disorientation, and wrestle with problems they can't resolve without adult help. Academic demands, peer pressure, and problems in their home life are some of the root causes that contribute to addictive behaviors. Parents and health practitioners alike must take the time to treat every child as a unique individual. When this doesn't happen, lives can be ruined.

10

THE "LOVE" WE LEARNED

Excessive habits and addictive behaviors are in essence "relationships" formed to fill an emotional need. These emotional needs are generally related in some way to the comfort and familiarity learned early on in life and defined and understood as "love" through the perceived and practical realities of parental and family life. Addictive personalities are needy and immature. Those who chase love idealize partners and internalize their partner's shortcomings. These behaviors are rooted in family-of-origin experiences and lead to unconscious romantic or sexual attraction to other distressed individuals similar in temperament to childhood caregivers and role models. Most people addicted to love relationships have problems that can be traced to unresolved childhood conflicts concerning autonomy and dependence, which inhibit our ability to develop a mature personality and form healthy romantic connections. Because American society so strongly emphasizes the importance of being in a romantic partnership, many people will allow themselves to be consumed by a romantic partner as a way to hide from their personal deficiencies and lack of emotional self-reliance. The most important love relationship that you'll ever have in life is with yourself. However, the need for acceptance makes someone actually further removed from themselves. There is cognitive dissonance and incongruence with someone who has learned to associate love with dysfunctional qualities yet is driven to love through fantasy and cultural ideals. It won't be until you really begin to unravel your subjective world that you can properly choose the right relationship to support both your own and your partner's growth and potential.

> Diane is a thirty-seven-year-old teacher who spends many weekly hours on Internet dating sites and Tinder, convinced she'll finally be happy once she marries the right man. Each new encounter fills her with a sense of hope and comfort, but the relationships usually fizzle out after a short time because of her attraction to emotionally aloof men who take advantage of her desperation. Diane seeks love and approval from every man she dates by being overly nurturing during the honeymoon phase of the relationship. As time progresses, she becomes less trusting and eventually sabotages the relationship by exhibiting unpredictable emotional outbursts and making false accusations—thereby driving away men who might have been good for her.

> Todd is a forty-two-year-old accountant who has never been married or involved in a long-term relationship. He's quick to fall in love and fall out of it even quicker. Todd is sad and needy for what he feels he truly desires: a loving wife and family. Unfortunately, his pattern of falling in love, getting scared of intimacy, and then moving on to the next woman appears to be a way of avoiding his own fears of abandonment and engulfment. After each relationship ends, Todd feels empty and lonely for a while before resolving to continue his search.

A person's need to be "in love" can become very addictive. In many ways, love is more addictive than anything else. People become addicted to love because they crave love, approval, and validation, and fear being alone. A love relationship becomes addictive in an unhealthy way when you continue to tolerate the other person's inappropriate and abusive behaviors instead of leaving. Each partner gets reinforcement when things are going well, and is reinforced by their attempts to avoid and hide from the bad aspects of their interaction. Hence the expression, "There's a thin line between love and hate." Many couples develop neurotic behavior patterns of making up by engaging in sex and temporarily being sweet with each other to relieve the emotional distress of arguing all the time. They're unable to leave a dysfunctional relationship because they become addicted to the hope of returning to the early stages of the romance where everything seemed so perfect. They become psychologically dependent on this pattern and will experience symptoms similar to chemical withdrawal if one or both has the courage to leave. The neurotic love relationship and its eventual termination produce the same highs and subsequent withdrawal symptoms as addictions to alcohol and drugs.

Often people in love forget they need to be mature, appropriate, and respectful toward one another. The saying "you hurt those you love the most" is not a license to act-out. You must learn to monitor your neurotic behavior patterns. The inability to do so creates emotional distress for both partners. You know you're being controlled by your unconscious when you lack self-control. It's a sign of immaturity.

Addictive behavior is learned and arises partly out of our need for love, approval, and validation. Early childhood experiences involving our parents or adult caregivers shape and form our attachment needs. We all yearn to belong and feel connected via close, enduring relationships. And yes, interpersonal connections are critical for our species' survival. But you must be aware of your subjectivity and how you cognitively and emotionally are processing your perceived and practical realities. Once you become more curious about the quality and content of your thinking, you can learn how to become more mindful and self-compassionate. Otherwise, you're merely obsessed, needy, and dependent on selective choice-making. A person who was abused during the formative years grows up with deficits involving trust and control and is more likely to become caught up in addictive romantic relationships. Because unresolved emotional problems are contributing factors to addictive behaviors, you should know about three relevant theories to help you understand how your brain is initially hardwired by early life experiences.

Object Relations Theory comes from the realm of psychology called psychodynamics, and asserts that early childhood experiences with primary caregivers have a powerful influence on adult relationships. For example, if children are neglected, abused, or fail to gain adequate love at home, they internalize these experiences and learn to be distrustful and emotionally dissociated from their primary caregivers. Such children will grow into adults who are unconsciously attracted to people who are similarly emotionally unavailable. Addictive behaviors are used to numb emotional distress, and can usually be traced to these early experiences.[1]

In a similar way, Attachment Theory, based upon the work of John Bowlby and Mary Ainsworth, suggests that our relationships as adults are influenced by our early attachment bonds, such as being cuddled and touched.[2] The famous studies by Harry Harlow demonstrated that when hungry and in distress, baby monkeys preferred the comfort of a soft touch even to being fed.[3] Insecure attachments in childhood induce adulthood depression and anxiety. These emotional states are preconditions for the development of addictive behaviors—and also foster a sense of helplessness.

Lastly, Learned Helplessness is a theory by Martin Seligman, who studied how people react to failure or frustration when they're unable to attain a goal.[4] Psychologically healthy people know that failure and rejection—though certainly unpleasant—are to be expected in life, and can even motivate us toward positive growth and change. However, others become pessimistic and gloomy after failure or rejection, and view their efforts as inevitably ineffective and therefore pointless. This attitude leads them to demean themselves as being worthless. They habitually see the glass as half empty and fall prey to negative feelings and thoughts. The facet of AA and twelve-step treatment approach that mandates the self-admission of powerlessness as a requirement for recovery actually reinforces learned helplessness among group members.

Trust and control issues originate in childhood. Erik Erikson's stages of psychosocial development outline the stages of *trust versus mistrust* and *autonomy versus doubt*—patterns which establish children's sense of self and their feelings of confidence, independence, and self-esteem. As previously stated, longitudinal studies show that children's personality at age seven is similar to their adult personality at age twenty-seven and even twenty years after that. This finding suggests that early childhood development not only forms the basis of our personality and susceptibility to mental challenges, but also contributes to the learned behavior that's enacted in adult relationships. The seminal psychological thinker Sigmund Freud created theories of human development which depicted how early learned behaviors can lead to addictive adult relationships. For Freud, the developmental stage between three and six years old is a time of sexual identity formation. He contended that boys compete with their father for maternal affection in a process he termed the Oedipus complex. We may have rightfully discarded much of Freud's thinking today, but clearly these early connections between the child and opposite-sex parent have merit.

How do I mean? Namely that the opposite-sex parent becomes the first idealized love relationship that a developing human experiences. For a woman, her father is her male role model and the man to whom all future men will be compared. Let's assume that when you were a little girl between three and six years old, your father was not around. Maybe he was divorced from your mother or passed away, or was away working all the time, or was simply neglectful. Perhaps he was often present at home, but was physically or verbally abusive. In either case, these early experiences have come to shape your personality and your ideas about relationships with men. A woman will search for her father figure her entire life if he was emotionally unavailable when she was in this early developmental period. She may unconsciously attract men who are emotionally distant in the same way. She may seek out idealized men with power and social significance whom she doesn't even like to attach herself to his identity and as a way to compensate for the early loss of healthy bonding with her idealized father.

Such psychological traits as the fear of abandonment, people-pleasing, and equating love with negative emotions and a disordered personality, are all rooted in early childhood experiences and particularly effected by trauma, abuse, and neglect. The brain's neural architecture is being created during traumatic childhood experiences to make seeking love and approval from dysfunctional people seem normal. The adult relationships we form provide unconscious familiarity with our family of origin role models. What often follows therefore is an adaptation to emotional abuse, idealization and devaluation, projection, and other survival skills necessary to cope with trauma and the accompanying guilt and shame which becomes imprinted during childhood and continued in romantic adult relationships. When imprinted in this way, a person becomes easily attracted to other disordered personality types—seduced by the loving, sweet nature they seek in a mate—and then addicted to the emotional roller coaster of abuse and reconciliation that often follows.

It's not surprising that people who attend AA or twelve-step meetings often mention the familial-like bond that's shared among group members. This groupthink resembles their painful family of origin dynamic, something which feels comfortable and familiar on an unconscious level. Many of these individuals are still trying to find themselves and haven't come to terms with childhood difficulties and the resulting fragile sense of self which they possess. Since such people are triggered by childhood memories and play out these dynamics in adulthood, it makes little sense for them to seek a romantic relationship when they haven't yet been able to make the learned associations of this dynamics consciously.

Love dependency is very real. It is more prevalent in American society than most people realize. People use romantic relationships to avoid real adulthood. Many men and women unconsciously look to be "parented" and are attracted to their partners in an attempt to receive the attention that was withdrawn by caregivers at some point during their childhood development. Thus, individuals who develop addictive behavior often show signs of arrested emotional development. Many psychological theories assert that people who are more inclined to chase love, approval, and validation failed to satisfy their emotional needs adequately in childhood. This affects their subjective experiences and reinforces low self-esteem, low self-worth, ruminations, and the impression that the world is unsafe and threatening. One way an adult can defend against basic anxiety is by repressing it and covering it up with an addictive relationship. For addictive behaviors can be viewed as an attempt to mount a defense against severe emotional instability.

Relationship chemistry refers to how you're attracted to someone on an unconscious, biological level—through your genetic makeup and the unconscious stored responses of past learning. When we say we have "chemistry" with someone, we really do. Love triggers the neurotransmitter dopamine in the brain and the hormone oxytocin. Testosterone in men and estrogen in women are chemical hormones that provide sexual attraction; dopamine provides intense feelings of love for each person and the hormones oxytocin and vasopressin in both partners help facilitate emotional bonding.[5] You know you're being driven by your unconscious mind and hormones when—despite big, obvious problems in your relationship—you believe you have great chemistry and avoid the real work to sustain a healthy connection or successfully end it. One can witness this pattern with many men and women by observing their choice of a romantic partner which usually reflects their emotional set-point at a particular time in their life.

Addictive love relationships can be far more debilitating emotionally and physically than other addictive behaviors. Many people who develop chronic stress and anxiety in a romantic relationship will turn to addictive behaviors to distract themselves from the pain of knowing they must get out. If you're a woman, you'll justify how he's emotionally distant and sometimes abusive; you may even think he's cheating on you, but tolerate it because you may be too afraid or not have the means to actually break free. How often is that the case—but at the same time, she's taking painkillers, eating or drinking excessively, and is generally unhappy, yet still doesn't make the connection between the two situations? Similarly, a man will say, "My girlfriend puts me down all the time and flirts with my friends, but the sex is the best I've ever had and I can't give that up." It's no surprise that he's drinking too much and overeating as well. It works both ways. Physical intimacy has tremendous impact and power. Unless both partners continually cultivate the qualities and requirements necessary for a healthy union, addictive and destructive behaviors can take over.

Most people are dependent on romantic relationships because as humans we're social animals. Research shows that when people are asked what missing element would bring them the most happiness and satisfaction in life, the majority answers that it's a happy love relationship—most important than anything else including wealth. We all have a basic need to be heard, seen, and acknowledged as being a significant, unique person who matters. But we often waste a lot of our time and energy—and compromise our own dignity—in seeking that fulfilling relationship. This quest takes us away from our true selves and reinforces the wrong thinking and behaviors that are being used to gain love in the first place. Love is healthy and life affirming only when both partners possess an authentic emotional life. This is a vastly different situation from pursuing love relationships for calculating reasons or because you feel powerless.

For example, a woman might marry a particular man because she seeks comfort and financial security. She tells herself she'll *learn* to love him, but she'll never be happy because she's not connected in an authentic way. Likewise, a man may marry a particular woman he's not compatible with emotionally simply for her physical beauty—because he craves the validation he gets from society by having a "trophy" wife. In such scenarios, seeking love for the wrong reasons or to compensate for perceived personal shortcomings can become addictive. All addictive behaviors related to love relationships are ways to increase the perception of happiness and reduce emotional distress. We're all looking for contacts with other people because we thrive for social interactions. That's why you'll hear some people say that they have a relationship with the alcohol, the drug, or the food to which they're addicted—because in many ways it's like a romantic relationship with another person. On some level it is temporarily fulfilling emotional needs.

You need to personally evolve first in order to attract someone who's really more emotionally available, serious, and committed. If you bring emotional instability into a relationship and the other person brings it as well, neither of you can change the other's self-determining nature. If there is a pattern of an ongoing need to date and chase for love, the common denominator for the lack of a healthy, quality outcome is you. As ironic as it sounds the attraction to drama and chaos is partly because of how someone learned and adapted to the intensity and unpredictability of growing up with emotional instability.

The same issue applies to men. Psychologically healthy, loving women are everywhere. The lonely single man must understand why he's not attracted to them. Was his mother abusive or abandoned him? Was she cold and dismissive? Is he unconsciously looking for a woman based on cultural stereotypes of youthful glamour, even though such women are often demanding and unpredictable? Our brain and its neural networks have been programmed since childhood based on our negative perceived, confusing formative experiences. This is why people are constantly attracted to "bad boys" and "crazy girls" all the while asking themselves and their friends: where are all the quality people? They are looking for love in all the wrong places.

Research studies on unconscious attraction confirm that a lot of our relationships—whether they're romantic, social, or work related—are emotionally similar to relationships in our early formative years. If your mom or dad was abusive, it should be no surprise that, twenty years later, you put up with an abusive boss, boyfriend, girlfriend, husband, or wife. You must make that connection and become aware of this tendency within yourself. If your mom or dad was emotionally distant, guess what? Your husband or your wife is likely to be emotionally distant. We always think that we're not going to be attracted to anyone like our parents if they hurt us emotionally while we were growing up. Unfortunately, the reality is that those undesirable traits are precisely the ones that pull us toward particular romantic partners. The connection we feel to our parents is natural. Parents can serve as positive role models, instilling traits in us that we value throughout our lifetime.

However, we can also create what Dr. Robert Firestone termed as a "fantasy bond" with our parents—an illusion of connection that aligns us with those who raise us and causes us to identify with them in ways that are negative as well as positive.[6] No person is perfect. Firestone declared that, "Even the best parents are only attuned to their children about 30 percent of the time. This is why it's important for us to recognize the ways that we've negatively adapted to the damaging side of those who cared for us as children. Once we identify how we shield ourselves from our past, we can separate from the internalized parents in our head and move forward as independent individuals, consciously adopting traits we respect and rejecting those that hurt us."[7]

Best-selling relationships author Harville Hendrix cautions, "Many people have a hard time accepting the idea that they've searched for partners who resemble their childhood caretakers. They've told themselves, 'I'll never marry a drunkard like my father,' or 'There's no way I'm going to marry a tyrant like my mother.' But no matter what their conscious intentions, most people are attracted to mates who have their childhood caretakers' positive and negative traits, and typically, the negative traits are more influential."[8]

This dynamic functions in subtle ways that can be difficult to identify. For example, if your mother was an uneducated Catholic woman with brown hair, brown eyes, and five feet tall and never attended college, even if you marry a Protestant woman who is five ten, well-educated, with green eyes and red hair doesn't mean she's not like your mother. Your wife may be demanding, just like your mother. Your wife may get impatient with you a lot, just like your mother. Your wife may be very critical and judgmental just like your mother. But like your mother who loved you, this behavior is what you have learned to accept as love to you. The value in identifying the tendency to re-create the negative dynamics of family of origin relationships is very valuable to changing learned behavioral patterns.

I have coached people who have been exposed to the AA or twelve-step culture and tell me their sponsor reminded them of their father, in good ways and bad. When people find comfort in this support offered, there is a transference that goes on between people. Most are sharing similar difficult childhood experiences, demons, and family dynamics. In many cases, they were the "identified patient" in their family while growing up; this is a term counselors use to describe the person in a dysfunctional family who's unconsciously selected by other family members to act-out the family's inner conflicts as a diversion from seeing the whole truth and correcting it. This person is the split-off (confused and self-destructive) carrier of the often transgenerational unhealthy habits, attitudes, and tolerated behaviors in the family.

Such individuals have a greater likelihood of addictive behaviors and are attracted to each other like a moth to a flame. They can be plentiful-ly found in the AA or twelve-step culture. They share similar stories and beliefs about their problems—and incorrectly assume that the under-standing they receive from other similarly affected group members will help them with their own problems. But sharing does not improve upon the quality of someone's thinking or their long-term positive well-being. To change the undesirable behavior, the support needs to come from the reinforcement of someone's independence.

There's definitely something to be said about unconscious attraction. You're driven by your unconscious when you believe that you have a soul mate and that finding this person is of paramount importance. To be sure, the soul mate concept is interesting—but also somewhat idea-listic. Why? Because generally those who believe in a single soul mate are coming from a place of fear and vulnerability. If you've been in a series of love relationships that didn't work out because the mutual attraction arose from strong unconscious needs, it's doubtful *the universe* will suddenly bring you a wonderful, healthy relationship. Rather, you'll likely attract someone who's comparable to you with a similar inability to emotionally self-regulate and who possesses unrealistic ex-pectations. Your match won't be your idealized version of the perfect mate—but a match to where you are in your life at the time you meet that person.

The soul mate search produces anxiety. It's an externalized ideal for happiness. Unhappiness suggests the need to fill an emotional void. You'd be better off spending your time developing your character, understanding your values, and resolving your underlying problems. Only then will you find the partner who will complement the new, healthier you. A related issue is that many people mistake an intense honeymoon phase of the relationship as proof of the validity of their romantic ardor. They reason that "this must be destiny"—and will often marry on mere infatuation, instead of considering character, emotional compatibility, life goals, and other important, enduring matters. When the honeymoon is inevitably over, one or both partners will rationalize that this person "must not really have been my soul mate." And the search continues.

It's unconscious attraction that propels us into relationships with people who aren't good for us. Romantic relationships can cause stress and create preconditions for other addictive behaviors. Once again, much of this behavior is dictated by learning and has become unconsciously stored and automatically reactive. But you can change these behavioral choices by becoming conscious of why you do things.

Here is an interesting exercise. Write down all the significant relationships you've ever had that were mature, appropriate, and respectful, as equally committed to the betterment of the other person as they were to you. These are relationships where you enjoyed a satisfactory amount of emotional availability, meaningful communication, and a sense of consistent joy, happiness, and life satisfaction. Relationships that were fulfilling and drama free. Relationships where there was an appreciation for one another, respect, gratitude, generosity, and kindness. Now describe how your relationships really are. Do your real relationships match these same qualities?

Now compare how you describe your current romantic relationships with your emotional connection and experiences growing up with your parents, siblings, and other family of origin members. Do you find similarities? Can you make the associations? This is what you're actually attracted to—and why your relationships all seem to turn out the same way. This is why you remain in a state of distress over your romantic relationships. In a sense, you have learned to seek out love only as it feels comfortable and familiar to you no matter how emotionally unstable you become.

As with any addictive behavior the goal is to seek out stimulation which is pleasurable and remove emotional distress. In love relationships, we often see that as time goes by the pleasure diminishes but the dependency on the other person may increase. Emotional pain occurs when the person (drug) is not around. One becomes dependent on the safety and security of a partner's proximity and may find it difficult to handle long periods apart. People in love relationships often suffer from painful withdrawal symptoms when a breakup occurs. For many people trapped in addictive love relationships much of their reasoning for remaining together is because of their fear of the unknown and their desire to avoid the withdrawal experience.

In this view of learned behavior and relationship formation let's compare alcohol dependency with being addicted to love:

1. They both feature a lack of control but are continued despite potentially adverse consequences. The heavy drinker loses a job or gets arrested. The love obsessed may not be able to think, eat, sleep, or work effectively.
2. They both create an obsession and a preoccupation. The heavy drinker spends much of the day thinking about drinking. Someone who is obsessed with love will be thinking constantly about the other person.
3. They both produce tolerance. A heavy drinker can drink so much alcohol it does not even provide any actual pleasure anymore. Someone who focuses on love relationships needs to love even more intensely to maintain the excitement, pleasure, and euphoria created in the brain that existed at the beginning of the relationship.
4. The heavy drinker will experience painful physical and emotional withdrawal symptoms when drinking is suddenly stopped. The person obsessed with love will experience cognitive, emotional, and physical problems when the other person withdraws. Both will often experience chronic stress, anxiety, and depression, while physically they may experience fatigue, headaches, aching muscles, or stomach and back pain.

If we learn from our experiences in life, we'll see that in some situations we're able to cope well—and in others we're not. You're surely capable of learning the proper communication skills, coping skills, and problem-solving skills that are necessary to make conscious behavioral choices which are part of maintaining a healthy romantic relationship. If you're already in an addictive relationship, you can make changes to function in a healthier way. If you and your partner came from similar emotionally unstable families in which trauma, abuse, neglect, abandonment, or divorce were common, the challenge in the relationship is to remain aware that you both probably have problems concerning trust and control. Therefore, unless one—and eventually both of you— breaks the habit of attempting to control the other, you actually maintain the problem. Unconsciously you're attracted to it, because it's another crack at getting the love, approval, and validation from mom and dad that you needed. Consciously though, it causes many problems because you're both conditioned to react in undesirable ways when someone else attempts to control you. *This reactance is learned.* It also contributes to neuroticism. Because humans need to love and be loved, and since all addictive behaviors are essentially relationships used to fill emotional needs, you could say in a sense that a distressed person coping with life challenges through a preoccupation with certain behaviors is searching for an authentic identity. But such a person has learned to hide behind the curtain in fear of self-discovering this identity and this relationship with oneself.

11

SUBJECTIVE WELL-BEING: THE GOAL OF ALL POSITIVE OUTCOMES

In treating those challenged by their human experiences and who have learned to adapt to their environmental stressors through the reinforcement of an excessive habit or an addictive behavior, a positive outcome needs to include an improvement in the individual's subjectivity and subjective experiences. Subjective well-being is how we experience our own quality of life both cognitively and emotionally. This quality, or lack thereof, is more useful in explaining why a wealthy, well-known, and successful person or a poor, unknown, and unemployed person can self-destruct and self-sabotage with abusive behaviors. Subjective well-being also takes into account our values and how we prioritize meaning in our life. These values are essentially unrelated to wealth, education, or other external factors that give the appearance of happiness. Subjective experiences are unique to each individual and cannot be objectively reduced; nobody knows what's really going on inside another person's mind. Because conventional treatment focuses on an abstinence-only approach and views the problem and its solution as a one-size-fits-all condition, it fails to recognize each person as a unique individual. This is why the AA or twelve-step treatment approach is limited with an abstinence-only mindset, because just being abstinent does not change subjectivity. True joy, happiness, and life satisfaction usually can't be experienced with a life philosophy based on being powerless, diseased, and needing lifelong management. Many AA or twelve-step members share a success in remaining abstinent for a specific period of time, yet may still have not learned anything new to help with coping, problem solving, and social skills. Rather than learning new information and expanding their subjectivity that would effectuate growth and change, the problems are reinforced by deficit-based language and the oversimplification of an abstinence-only measure of effective and successful treatment to this disregard of the individual's overall subjective well-being. This is neither healthy nor wise.

> By all outward appearances Alex is very happy. He's a forty-year-old corporate manager, has been married for ten years, has two healthy children, and zero financial worries. After initial experiences at parties, Alex began using cocaine regularly and found that it quickly became addictive. His close friends couldn't understand how Alex could even think of sabotaging the perfect life he seemed to have. Alex finally admitted to his therapist that he has never really been in love with his wife and has been unhappy for most of their marriage. He realized that his cocaine use was a way for him to "escape" because he didn't know how to handle the guilt of breaking up his family by seeking a divorce, especially since his wife is usually a pleasant, easygoing person.

> Megan is a twenty-seven-year-old woman who lives with her parents and is unhappy with her life. She has no job, few friends, and spends her days watching TV and eating. She's overweight and physically unhealthy for her age. One day Megan received an email from a former high school sweetheart who said he was coming to town for a new job assignment in a few months. Megan's desire to look attractive for him accessed her motivation to start exercising and eating better. Each day, she looked forward to his arrival. When they finally met, she felt happy for the first time in years. From that point forward, she knew that she no longer needed the temporary fix of food to feel satisfied—and that her long-term happiness really came from the excitement she got from setting goals and following through on things she planned for her life—which she resolved to do daily from then on.

Subjective well-being is the unique way you view yourself and your life circumstances—how you see the world and the thoughts that are specific to you. This always goes back to the quality of your thinking. Only you know what you're really thinking and how your circumstances are affecting you at any given moment. When we talk about addictive behaviors, everyone has individualistic experiences. Nobody really knows the specific reasons for why you're acting out in an addictive way. This notion is important to understand because we see rich and famous people who—despite having all the things that would seemingly make someone happy—are actually miserable, addicted, and checking in and out of rehabs. Why? Because for them, subjectively, their life is not so wonderful. They're not truly happy; they don't experience a great deal of life satisfaction and are challenged by emotional instability. As surprising as that might sound to the average person who thinks that money, fame, and power automatically generate happiness, this is the reality. At the end of the day, we are all human and there is really no place for your thoughts to hide.

What makes subjective well-being so important? You must realize, for example, that if you're seeking help for a drinking problem, and you're told that you have a disease, are powerless to cure it, need lifelong support, and your primary priority in life must be to remain abstinent from alcohol, how could that improve the quality of your thinking? If you remain abstinent for six months, two years, or five years—that's all well and good in my view especially if your drinking has been causing harm to yourself or others. But if you still experience a daily uneasiness, anxiousness, and apprehension, and if you have not actually learned new ways to widen the frame of your independent thinking, each day you will reinforce these experiences. They become your mindset. You escape by working, by playing, or by a variety of different habits and more compulsive behaviors but, at the end of the day, you are alone inside your head by yourself with your personal narration. Just being abstinent will not make you happy if there is not a concerted effort to also acknowledge, embrace, and rethink your neurotic behaviors. How do you feel in terms of your life and what's going on in it? Do you feel empowered and fulfilled? Do you have a sense of direction, meaning, and purpose? Are you excited about the future and all its possibilities? Why might learning new things about addictive behavior that you didn't know before help you? Why might widening the frame of your thinking and beliefs to gain access to new learning opportunities be desirable to you?

In the book, *Happiness: Unlocking the Mysteries of Psychological Health*, the authors write:

An individual's subjective well-being is often related to some degree to their objective circumstances, but it also depends on how people think and feel about these conditions. Subjective well-being encompasses people's life satisfaction and their evaluation of important domains of life such as work, health and relationships. Even if the circumstances of your life in one or more areas are not what you want them to be, you can still have a positive attitude while taking actions to change unwanted conditions. This is important because how one thinks about his or her life also plays a part in determining one's subjective well-being.[1]

In psychology, subjective well-being focuses on the major areas of joy, happiness, life satisfaction, and neuroticism. Someone who worries frequently about what others are thinking and how it could negatively impact his life has a higher degree of neuroticism. Think of some of Woody Allen's characters in his earlier films: people who are habitually fearful and stressed for a variety of real or imagined reasons, and often moody and mildly depressed. "Neuroticism is a fundamental personality trait characterized by anxiety, moodiness, and jealousy. Individuals who score high on a neuroticism scale are more likely than the average person to experience feelings such as anger, guilt, or a depressed mood. They respond more poorly to stress and are more likely to interpret ordinary situations as threatening and minor frustrations as hopelessly difficult. They are often self-conscious and shy and they may have trouble controlling urges and delaying gratification."[2]

When you examine your level of joy, happiness, life satisfaction, and neuroticism—and where you are on a scale of measuring them—you don't want to be self-deceptive. An authentic awareness of your personal narration is a good first course of action. Listen to yourself. What do you sound like? By doing so, you can be more inclined to learn to develop the necessary coping strategies to deal with chronic stress, depression, low self-esteem, and anxiety. If you don't have a relatively consistent level of life satisfaction and an absence of mood swings and tension, you'll never feel happy and fulfilled—no matter how long you remain abstinent or how many possessions and career achievements you attain.

Psychologist Albert Bandura gave us the theoretical construct of self-efficacy. It's the strength or measure of your belief in your ability to complete tasks and reach goals in life. Self-efficacy affects every area of human endeavor. By determining the beliefs people hold regarding their power to affect situations, it strongly influences their ability to face challenges competently and make effective choices. These effects are particularly apparent, and compelling, with regard to behaviors affecting your emotional and physical health.[3]

The idea behind self-efficacy is that when you decide you want to do something (lose that extra twenty pounds, master a new language) and then you actually accomplish it, you'll continue to do it (eat healthier and physically exercise, speak regularly in the new language) because it brings you feelings of well-being and an increased sense of personal power. Conventional old-school thinking places too much emphasis on being totally abstinent and not enough on teaching how to learn healthier ways to think and, by doing so, create the mindset to tackle current and past problems for people to experience self-efficacy and subjective well-being.

In my view, the individual's "depression" is a symptom of underlying problems and the addictive behavior is a coping strategy used to deal with the depression based on subjective experiences. The individual feels relief when he/she drinks and receives reinforcement. When someone is "dual-diagnosed" and advised to remain abstinent, if he/she doesn't deal with the underlying reasons for the depression—which induced drinking too much in the first place—true happiness and life satisfaction will always remain elusive. The person may successfully remain sober, but still remain challenged by his/her thinking. In this regard, the word "sober" is also conventionally misused. It has become synonymous with abstinence, but the actual meaning of sober is not being drunk or measurably affected by drinking and/or drugging. This misuse of language is problematic because someone who believes he/she is powerless is obviously not going to be able to stop eating, shopping, texting, using a mobile phone, using the Internet, looking for love, and having sex. If these are problematic in an addictive way, the goal is to reduce the severity of the problem producing a remission. The remission of addictive behaviors allow for the development of self-efficacy and the improvement of the subjective experience.

This is why for helping professionals and the individual that an understanding and appreciation for subjective well-being is very valuable. This is a much better assessment to use in providing a course of action that is appropriate for the individual. This will help gain a real-time perspective on an individual's subjective life.

I would still maintain that for the small percentage of people that remain abstinent through years of AA support are demonstrating their ability to make a conscious behavioral choice, and therefore their self-control. Although limiting in widening the frame of human experiencing through creative thinking and new learning, those that subscribe anecdotally to AA's helpfulness in managing their lives within this framework have also reinforced this subjective mindset. Nevertheless, most of the steps involve turning your "will and life" over to God, making lists of your character defects and shortcomings, and naming people whom you've harmed and to whom you need to apologize is old-school thinking. It doesn't go far enough for most people to achieve subjective well-being. The AA or twelve-step program puts the problem outside of you by saying you're diseased and powerless and that only a higher power (something outside yourself) can help you with your problem. You know yourself better than anyone else. Therefore, you must be your own agent for change in your own time and when you want to access your own motivation to do so in dealing with your problems and searching for solutions. Your thought processes are known only to you: so how can anyone say what's best for you, what to think, how to behave, and what to believe?

Subjective well-being should be a major part of what is considered a positive outcome for any treatment approach deemed "effective." If you're challenged by certain problematic behaviors, address the quality of your thinking. Let's suppose that after a long period of problem drinking you have finally stopped with the help of a conventional rehab. At the same time, you now are dependent on an antidepressant drug, you drink five cups of coffee a day, smoke cigarettes or eat lots of sugar, and are unable to control your anger and discontent. Do you honestly believe that you've achieved treatment success? How about if you regularly experience drama and chaos in your personal relationships, are depressed, and have low self-esteem, but remain abstinent from alcohol? Would you consider this treatment success? I wouldn't.

Don't assume that your treatment outcome has been successful just because you stopped a behavior until you have learned something new about yourself. It's like a relationship. The only common denominator in someone's short-lived or patterned dysfunctional relationships, is you. Many people do not take the time to learn from their experiences and so they merely continue the pattern wondering why they can't find love. So too, for every time that you are able to moderate, wean off, or completely discontinue a behavior it provides the opportunity to learn about yourself and the ways in which your thinking has kept you stuck.

If conventional treatment is based on a literal disease like cancer, could being told you had cancer with no possibility of ever being cancer free again ever help you to feel happy? If you hear a lot of people sharing sad stories about the "wreckage of their past": their bad drinking/drugging episodes, the people they've hurt, how badly they felt, etc., how would that improve the quality of your thinking and your subjective experience? This belief in a shared, common core of self-destructive tendencies—along with belief in powerlessness over a disease that only a higher power can ameliorate—connects each individual in a way that does not enhance their subjective experience. Yes, those strictly adhering to an abstinence-only mindset applaud one another when they announce how many days, months, or years in a row they've been completely abstinent, but this limited definition of a positive outcome is not the same as possessing subjective well-being.

Subjective well-being is also important for our physical health. Studies show that subjective well-being is associated with positive health outcomes, such as greater resistance to disease and lower mortality rates. Further studies indicate that happier people are more likely to have healthier immune systems than those chronically unhappy. In addition, poor physical health is associated with the presence of negative emotions like anxiety, anger, and depression. Subjective well-being is important because it's central to our physical, psychological, and spiritual well-being—which taken all together basically defines the concept of wellness. The World Health Organization finds that, "health is a state of complete physical, mental and social well-being, and not merely the absence of disease and infirmity."[4]

In addition, studies show a direct connection between health status and specific psychological factors. For example, stress levels have been directly linked to susceptibility to the common cold. The implication is that excessive stress causes negative emotionality, which then disturbs the nervous system and compromises the immune system—thus increasing the likelihood of catching a cold. Finally, subjective well-being has been shown to lower stress hormones and blood pressure, as well as raise endorphin levels which increase positive moods.

Physical health directly affects changing moods and attitudes. For example, if someone is in a positive emotional state, they are more likely to also be calm, rational, and self-confident. They are more likely to be optimistic and invigorated, and feel physically fit and strong. This is a desired state. When someone receives a perceived challenge it is likely they may get anxious or uncomfortable—and they may become overwhelmed by bodily sensations of stress, and temporarily develop somatic problems. For example, you get a dull headache, or your muscles begin to ache. Mentally, you don't feel as optimistic. You are no longer as logical and rational for the time being. You don't feel as strong physically and may actually question your overall health. You may have irrational worries now about your body. Your thinking begins to unravel.

These are transient states. However, the shift in bodily sensations and vulnerability are readily apparent. I'm not prone to illness and rarely get sick. But when I do, in most instances, the cold or flu was precipitated by a stressful situation—which apparently compromised my immune system and made me more vulnerable to viruses.

Physical activity reduces chronic stress that debilitates the mind. Interestingly enough, a young athlete that I was coaching through some personal challenges told me that he found a correlation between his mental outlook and the quality of his workouts that affected his subjective well-being. For example, if he was in a positive emotional state when he worked out, he said he felt everything was good in his life and that he had a productive day regardless of what had occurred at work. He was relaxed. His thinking was enhanced and he felt content. But on other days when he was in a negative emotional state, he sometimes injured himself by approaching the activity without the same enthusiasm. Also, when he was stressed, worried, or pessimistic, he said he even ran differently. It changed his running mechanics. In turn, these led to his feelings of discouragement. In this way the brain demonstrates how one's subjectivity can influence cognitive, emotional, and physical well-being.

Optimism (the belief that good things will come in the future) and an internal locus of control (the belief that you have control over your life path and internal states) are vitally related to subjective well-being. The reason why optimism works is because your thoughts about your future possibilities affect your current circumstances, in that by expecting to do well, you'll work more effectively and continue to strive for the goals you've set. But I see the future as not some distant time frame, rather in each passing moment. In each passing moment you change your "past" by immediately rethinking, reframing, or choosing to remove the experience from keeping you stuck. This takes mindfulness and will greatly improve upon your subjective well-being. Studies show that having a fulfilling work and social life, and a network of supportive family and friends, are strongly associated with subjective well-being. This may appear obvious, but someone that has work, family, and a social life may not think or believe they are fulfilling. They may not be having good subjective experiences in spite of outward appearances.

In his book, *Flourish*, Martin Seligman, pioneering researcher in the field of positive psychology affirmed that "The good life partly consists of five elements listed under the acronym PERMA: Positive emotion—tunable by writing down, every day at bed time, three things that went well and why, Engagement—tunable by preferentially using one's highest strengths to perform the tasks which one would perform anyway, Relationships—'I've always said that the most important thing in life is the cultivation of quality relationships. Everything is about relationships. Success in business, work, intimacy, friendship, family and even the self (the way you treat yourself is crucial) . . . is determined by the quality of your relationships.' Meaning—belonging to and serving something bigger than one's self and Achievement—determination is known to count for more than IQ."[5]

Seligman described psychologist Mihaly Csikszentmihalyi as a leading world researcher on positive psychology who cogently stated that, "Repression is not the way to virtue. When people restrain themselves out of fear, their lives are by necessity diminished. Only through freely chosen discipline can life be enjoyed and still kept within the bounds of reason."[6] *Flow* is a term advanced by Csikszentmihalyi, and in current psychological study refers to a mental state in which people are so completely absorbed in an activity that they lose consciousness of self and time. In sports, this condition is known as being "in the zone." One is so immersed in an activity that the degree of involvement and focus is extremely high. Flow can also be understood as when challenges equal the skill set necessary to successfully participate in an activity—yielding great satisfaction and well-being.

Psychologists today know that people who experience high challenges and have high skills are more likely to experience flow than those with high challenges but low skills: they'd be likely to experience anxiety. How about people with low challenges and high skills? They'll become bored. Finally, those with low challenges and low skills will become apathetic. The idea behind flow is that in this state, not only do people experience positive emotionality—but that the self-mastery and good feelings that result produce subjective well-being. To experience flow you need to change your thinking. Great athletes who seem to perform "unconsciously" at the most crucial moments in games are demonstrating being in the flow. It's also no secret that these same athletes are the ones with a great work ethic and high sport IQ.

Csikszentmihalyi contends that to experience flow, we need to find work and activities that are at or slightly above our skill level. The successful artist and the athlete continually raise their level of challenge, so that their performance improves. They have the ability to screen out distractions when necessary and focus their attention on the emotional and sensory qualities required for the activity. They also look for regular feedback and set goals by which they can monitor progress. These qualities of commitment and determination are seen in people that regularly experience flow. You can learn them for yourself if you make the commitment. What level of drive do you possess? Do you have an internal or external locus of control?

Individuals with a high internal locus of control believe that events in their lives originate from their own actions. For example, if a person with an internal locus of control doesn't perform well on a test, he would attribute it to a failure to study and prepare adequately. If this same person performed well on a test, the outcome would then be attributed to his decision to prepare and study. Likewise, if someone with a high external locus of control did poorly on the test, she might attribute the outcome to the confusing nature of the test questions. If she did well on a test, they might think the teacher used a grading scale or that they were lucky.

As I stated earlier, I teach college psychology classes for inner-city students—men and women of low socioeconomic status whose life distress is constant and who see a lot of addictive behaviors in their neighborhoods. At the same time, I do existential coaching for addictive behaviors with many people who are quite affluent and who have achieved significant career success. Interestingly enough, the reasons for difficulties to cope with their life challenges are usually the same. That is, people suffer similar problems psychologically and emotionally no matter who they are or where they come from. In both socioeconomic groups, individuals have failed to improve upon the quality of their thinking, they reinforce deficit-based language through their self-talk and they are not having good subjective experiences. These are internal states—and the sole territory of the individuals and their subjective well-being. Ultimately we're all alone in the world despite the many people in our lives including families and significant others. It's in our moments of self-reflection and mindfulness that we can embrace and appreciate our lives, the good, the bad, and the ugly.

This is why even using the new term "evidence-based" treatment needs clarification. What is the objective of treatment? Abstinence only? Is that the only measure of a successful outcome? It can't be. Individuals need to have a better experience of themselves. They need a fundamental shift in the language they use to describe themselves and their perceived and practical realities. They need to grow, change, and evolve in all areas of their life. When their relationship with themselves improves, their relationships with others will be better and their need to fill the void through learned coping behaviors can be replaced by healthier choices.

Behind subjective well-being is learning. Learning is an ongoing process. Thinking is a process which is a learned skill. We make assumptions and infer that people have "learned their lesson" when we observe a change in their undesirable behavior by something that has been imposed upon them. The problem, however, is that when we impose this through emotionally charged deficit-based language in an effort to change, control, or cure another person, we are not respecting or appreciating their autonomy nor are we recognizing their self-determining nature. Therefore, learning should not only be measured by observing desired outcomes but also through the overall improvement of someone's subjective well-being.

12

RETHINKING YOUR LIFE CHALLENGES AND EXPERIENCES

Life challenges and experiences are learned early on in life and become stored in the unconscious. When we are triggered by a stressor these stored experiences and reactions to them are activated automatically. The brain is an organ of social adaptation so early childhood environments shape and form the architecture of the brain's neural networks. Therefore, future environments either contribute to maintaining this brain adaptation or enhance and support the activation of the brain's neuroplasticity. We know that the fear center of the brain, the amygdala, is fully developed at birth but the ability to regulate it comes many years after. Each individual learns in their own subjective way how to deal with the problems in living their lives. This can produce chronic stress and anxiety that inhibits the ability to properly process cognitive and emotional experiences. This is a result of faulty connections in the circuits which regulate how the unconscious processes of the amygdala and the conscious processing of the prefrontal cortex activate or inhibit each other. In a sense, you could say that the brain is *biologically social* and that the first social experiences in life are fear based. As the brain is adapting to its environment it is learning how to perceive reality. This is why you could say that fear is our primary motivator. Early life experiences and how we regulate and process cognitive and emotional experiences shapes and forms our brain and our personalities. Addictive behaviors can be traced to the inability to regulate the stored emotions that were necessary in adapting to life challenges and experiences. The more serious the addictive behaviors are the more deeply rooted the underlying problems. Many of the emotional symptoms we deal with in everyday life are the direct result of these experiences—and include depression, anger, anxiety, and unhappiness, trauma, abuse, neglect, or simply the perception of not having gotten our needs met when we needed them. Many life experiences are cloaked in secrecy, shame, guilt, and other negative associations. The goal is to deconstruct the deficit-based language, and rewrite the personal stories and experiences to reprocess and integrate them into the brain and thus create new neural networks and new architecture. In this regard, empowering, encouraging, facilitating, supporting, and reinforcing someone's subjective growth and independence could actually be considered a "biological" approach to helping anyone with an addictive behavior.

> Kelly is a thirty-year-old artist and lesbian. She has been using me-thamphetamines and drinking excessively for some time. She has been led to believe that she has a disease and is powerless, but after proper coaching, Kelly realized that her problems were rooted in her feelings of shame left over from growing up in a conservative, rural town where her sexuality wasn't accepted. When Kelly learned that lesbian women are four times more likely to become addicted than heterosexual women, she clearly saw that she needed to embrace her sexuality and learn healthy ways to cope with life problems. Thus, she would no longer need to hide and self-medicate by abusing drugs and alcohol.

> Henry is a forty-four-year-old photographer addicted to pornography. He spends a lot of time on the Internet viewing pornography, sometimes even at work, and his interactions with real women are very awkward. Through coaching, Henry learned that the majority of people addicted to pornography were sexually abused as children. By revisiting his own childhood abuse experiences and rethinking them, he saw how his enjoyment of degrading sexuality involving women was directly linked to the unconscious anger he still felt toward his mother, who had belittled and shamed him when he was a boy. Henry overcame his preoccupation with Internet pornography, and over time, he began to establish healthier relationships with real women.

Addictive behaviors are human experiences. Because we all experience life differently, these behaviors often catalyzed by something in your past that still affects your present. It could be childhood abuse, neglect, abandonment, sexual abuse, or simply the perception that you were not getting your needs met. Many of your addictive behaviors are a coping response to emotional problems that need to be rethought with self-compassion for successful long-term outcomes to materialize in your life's key areas. Addictive behavior can even be a way of avoiding such problems—a means of escape, distraction, and avoidance. One can live for years distracted and misguided without ever scratching the surface of what's really behind the addictive behavior.

Unless you become mindful and embrace your unease by viewing distress as a directive to change your thinking, you'll be unable to regulate your emotions and thereby tainting your perceived and practical realities. If your parents were ineffective at providing you with good role modeling, coping skills, and problem-solving abilities, then your childhood has probably had a significant influence on how you see yourself, how you see others, and how others see you. If you're challenged by addictive behaviors, you need to rethink, reprocess, and integrate new learning to change your subjectivity. Otherwise, an arrested emotional development will occur because of the imprinting from an early age that induced you to assume the world is unsafe and threatening, causing a constant feeling of anxiety. What does this really mean? That people, situations, and interactions can make you feel uncomfortable, hyper-vigilant, or insecure. You attempt to repress this anxiety to avoid feeling it. Your addictive behaviors become your defense mechanism—a protection from your emotional insecurity maintained through the reinforcement of deficit-based language and in the inability to properly regulate emotions. The amygdala and your deficit-based language are controlling you.

You become overwhelmed when you're unable to attain a desired goal—such as a fulfilling career, financial stability, or a happy romantic relationship—and thus feel the need to escape unpleasant feelings and situations. So you have learned to act out addictively. But it gets worse. Your frustration with being unable to self-regulate and adapt to your environment manifests itself through chronic stress and anxiety, which creates more frustration—influencing your choices to abuse alcohol, drugs, or food to self-soothe. Many people who are challenged with addictive behavior avoid facing their life challenges and rethinking their prior experiences. Why? Because doing so is frightening. When those negative feelings arise, the urge to act out becomes intense because it has become the automatically learned default behavior.

For example, suppose someone grew up in a family environment that was filled with drama and chaos. The family dealt with their problems by fighting and arguing and never really resolved these problems. Now as an adult, whenever this individual experiences a conflict with coworkers or friends, wife or children, he's unable to resolve it in a calm, mature way; rather, he becomes angry and defensive. Since he lacks coping and problem-solving skills such as emotional regulation and good communication, he retreats to self-soothing through his default behaviors—perhaps involving drinking and drugging. He wants to avoid the unpleasant feelings elicited from conflict, ambivalence, cognitive dissonance, chronic stress, anxiety, and depression and so he learns that certain behaviors can temporarily dissipate these feelings.

Let's assume someone remains abstinent for several weeks, but becomes triggered by a stressor. The activation of the amygdala elicits fear and she may get angry because of the inability to regulate themselves emotionally. She may desire to avoid conflict, by blaming others, and feeling victimized. She may then act out. And the cycle repeats. Effectively treating this cycle means being aware of its existence, identifying the triggers and interrupting the behavior to make the associations between your present choices and your prior learning experiences. By not being aware of how you learned and to understand the associations between how the past influences the present, you will reinforce and maintain emotional disturbance. Even when the drugs and alcohol may have been put away, neither your subjectivity nor your coping ability may have changed. So you'll often remain stuck in a more adolescent phase of arrested development and have difficulty maturing out of it.

Life challenges and normal human experiences that lead to addictive behaviors are rarely the focus of AA and twelve-step meetings and other conventional treatment approaches. This is because dealing with symptoms (addictive behaviors) is much easier than respecting and appreciating subjective human experiences. In the June 2013 edition of *Alcoholism: Clinical and Experimental Research*, a team of researchers investigated the connection between childhood trauma and adult alcohol dependency. They compared two groups of men and women: the first had initially sought treatment for alcohol dependency and another group hadn't. Not only was childhood trauma, abuse, and neglect significantly more pronounced in men and women who were seeking help for alcohol abuse, but that the intensity of their drinking difficulties were directly correlated with the intensity of their childhood trauma. Those who had suffered greater emotional abuse and neglect during childhood reported higher adult levels of anxiety, depression, and anger. These findings suggest that genetics alone is inadequate to explain vulnerability to alcohol dependency. The same study also reported a connection between childhood trauma and impulsive behavior. Certainly, these findings support the alternative treatment options championed by more progressive providers—and historically resisted by disease model–based treatment approaches. [1]

Through self-discovery you focus on the strong link between your childhood dissatisfactions and longing and your present discomfort with your default behaviors. It's empowering to bring this link to full conscious awareness. Many people gaze back on their childhood convinced they had sufficient love because there was no obvious abuse and trauma. This view can mistakenly cause them to dismiss the link between their perceived unmet childhood needs and their current acting-out behaviors. In many homes without obvious signs of abuse or neglect, children can still be feel invisible, alone, confused, and not understood. From a developmental perspective, no matter how functional or less functioning a child's environment was, each child "downloads" their own perception of reality in their own way. This shapes and forms his/her brain's architecture, personalities, and subjectivity.

Let's reexamine the cognitive psychology theory of your dual processing/dual track mind. You have a conscious mind of which you're aware—your thoughts at any given moment, your surroundings, and so on. You also have an unconscious mind—involving things of which you're unaware and which you do automatically. The theory is that our mind is always processing information consciously and unconsciously at the same time. Acting on this information becomes automatic when it's unconscious and controlled when it's conscious. It also becomes part of our memory system. Memories of which we're aware are conscious (explicit) and memories of which we're unaware are unconscious (implicit).

Again, using the example of driving a car, when you first learn to drive a car you need to make a conscious effort to pay attention to avoid an accident. However, after time, you can literally drive from one place to another while perhaps daydreaming—and still get there because of your stored memories that automatically work without your conscious awareness. If you've been driving for a decade or longer, you may experience a feeling occasionally when you don't recall anything about your last two minutes of driving. It's a bit frightening in a way. Well, your unconscious mind was "driving" the car during that time. You were consciously aware that you were talking on the phone or changing the music, but at the same time you also turned left, avoided striking another car, and arrived at your predetermined destination—all controlled partly by your unconscious mind. Both processes were occurring at the same time. Hence, the dual-track theory. One brain, two minds, but all part of the living system, not a dualistic separation of mind and body.

Now, let's take the example of Jason, who is a problem drinker. On a conscious level, he craves a drink and chooses to enter a bar. This act is under Jason's control, it's a conscious choice. Remember, behaviors are learned therefore are chosen. However, once Jason starts to imbibe, he begins drinking one after another. In effect, Jason is in control of choosing to go to the bar to drink, but he has limited influence over his automatic, unconscious stored experiences and memories that keep him drinking alcohol once he starts. He then drinks heavily to the point of passing out. Conventional thinking would suggest that this is an example of Jason being powerless over alcohol once he starts drinking. But this theory disregards that such behavior is learned—therefore it can be unlearned and changed. Even when it appears you have no control, you're still propelled on both conscious and unconscious levels.

Medical researchers at Kaiser Permanente's Department of Preventative Medicine in San Diego found that patients who were losing the most weight in their weight loss program were also the ones most likely to drop out and quit. The researchers wondered why this was occurring: was it because these patients no longer needed the program? Further investigation revealed that the majority of dropouts didn't maintain their weight loss and returned to being challenged with their problems of overeating and obesity. Why did they quit if they were succeeding in the program? A deeper look revealed that overeating and obesity were used as self-soothing behaviors to cope with unresolved adverse child-hood experiences (ACE). In most cases, overeating was an unconscious behavior utilized as a protective solution to these unresolved childhood problems. How was it unconsciously protective? In many cases, the adverse childhood experiences involved sexual, physical, or emotional abuse. Patients unconsciously felt that a *relationship* with food was safer than developing intimate or nurturing relationships with people. The finding that most of the participants in the weight loss program had prior ACEs led Kaiser to collaborate with the Centers for Disease Control (CDC) to explore more intensely the link between childhood abuse and addictive behaviors.

Their study has involved over seventeen thousand middle-class Americans and produced over fifty research journal articles. Among the most significant findings was that two-thirds of the participants reported at least one ACE and more than one in five reported three or more ACEs. In addition, the higher a person's ACE score, the more that addictive behavior was utilized as a coping response. For example, as the number of ACEs increased, so too did the percentage of participants who met the criteria for alcohol use disorder. This massive study helps us to understand that the biological connection to brain changes is more useful to understand in the context of early social learning experiences. These experiences are real, diverse, and if left unaddressed, will continue to fuel the behavior that we're so eagerly seeking to manage or eliminate. [2]

Learning affects your sensory perceptions and how you interpret cues from your environment—actually shaping how you see and hear things—thereby influencing your daily thoughts and actions. It takes courage and determination to look at yourself and to consider how thoughts and beliefs are affecting your life in an undesirable way. But only if you want to. Understanding the origins of how your thoughts and beliefs influence your choices provides for new learning. We take our belief systems everywhere we go. Situations will continue to present themselves in repeat patterns until you become aware of the learned associations between the past and the present. You may be afraid of this process and the experiencing of intense emotions, but one thing is for sure, substances and behaviors used to avoid emotional distress are temporary and prescription drugs are still drugs that even in "therapeutic" levels are not correcting or fixing anything in spite of how they are marketed.

When we have a painful experience and are unable to cope with the unwanted feelings that accompany it, we often repress them—and drink too much, abuse drugs, binge eat—or just pretend that event didn't happen. It takes a lot of energy to keep powerful feelings of anger, sadness, and despair held in check. If you do so chronically, it will often lead to physical illness and an accelerated aging process. These emotions remain hidden within us until we allow ourselves to feel and release them. Embracing and acknowledging feelings through self-compassion is very beneficial. Cutting yourself off from your true feelings will affect all your relationships—and inhibit your ability to learn new ways of adapting to any environment with healthier thinking and making choices.

In a sense, when you have repressed emotions and have not embraced them, your acting-out behavior in the present moment is actually your learned unconsciously stored responses to past events. To address these emotional problems, you can ask yourself, "Why might acknowledging and embracing the origins of my emotional disturbances be a great learning opportunity?" Since you experienced many of these situations as a child and your personality and brain have been "hard-wired" by them, you need to "rewire" your brain by taking advantage of the brain's neuroplasticity. As mentioned earlier, neuroplasticity refers to changes in neural pathways and synapses which occur because of changes in behavior, environment, and thought processes that in turn affect neural processes. The brain is a social organ of adaptation and is not a physiologically static organ. [3]

Research now indicates that experiences can actually change both the brain's anatomy (physical structure) and physiology (functional organization). The role of neuroplasticity is increasingly recognized in studies of healthy emotional and social development, learning, memory, and recovery from brain damage. During most of the twentieth century, the consensus among neuroscientists was that brain structure is relatively unchangeable after early childhood. However, this belief has been decisively challenged by findings revealing that many aspects of the brain remain plastic (able to be changed) throughout adulthood. [4]

Neuroplasticity supports the viewpoint that a change in thinking can also induce neurological long-term change. In other words, the goal-directed process of changing negative thoughts to positive ones and visualizing beneficial outcomes can produce a change in a person's behavior and habitual thinking. Through mindful conscious effort, you can rethink past experiences, rewrite your own personal narrative, and using positive mental imaginary and other retraining techniques, you can actually change the brain and thus change your subjective reality. A "reprogramming" of your brain is thus possible, despite how your childhood learned behavior has influenced your adult choice-making decisions. This is informative because it suggests that addictive behavior is not simply reducible to a brain area or dopamine functions that are used to support the idea of *cause*, but rather is more suggestive that an individual's early learning experiences create the brain's architecture that makes an individual more vulnerable and susceptible to environmental stressors. In this way, rather than conceptualizing a dualistic separation where the brain is causing behavior to occur outside of one's control, it is of greater utility to view the mind, brain, and body as one living system. From this understanding, thoughts and new learning create new neural networks and consequently new behavior. We know from placebo studies that expectations and thinking has a direct effect on biology. If a placebo works to any extent it's not just a change in subjectivity but also in biology. In other words, if the theory is that an SSRI produces a chemical balance where there had been an *imbalance* by introducing serotonin into the brain and positively affecting mood, that's a biological occurrence. If the mood is positively affected by the placebo and it has a similar effect as the actual drug, this would imply that an individual's perception of reality based on subjectivity has significant biological influence. This would also suggest that either the placebo is producing a theorized chemical balance as well, or that the chemical imbalance may have very little to do with it. Either way you look at it, the subjective experience affects biology and is biology.

Rather than believing that you can't consume alcohol because "alcoholism" runs in the family, you have an allergy of the body, a chemical imbalance, a missing gene, a spiritual disease, or another label and that you are now rendered powerless, interpersonal biology and placebo studies demonstrate that you have the conscious ability to positively influence your brain activity and consequently curb your acting-out behaviors.

Think about how you learned. Perhaps you had many experiences of emotional or physical abuse and realized that you weren't in control. You weren't able to express your anger back then. You internalized these experiences, and they're now stored responses in the unconscious. Now you may choose to not drink or use drugs but still get angry very easily. When someone or something triggers you, your anger is projected outward because you're attempting to protect yourself from your perception of being harmed, overwhelmed, or threatened in a way that's similar to how you learned and experienced life as a child.

If you were honest with yourself, you would never say that you love your life and are very happy and then make the decision to self-destruct. I believe the dual diagnosis contributes to maintaining addictive behavior and reinforces dependency. For example, a person who is experiencing what we call depression is feeling helpless already. If they are told they are powerless too, is it any wonder why they have such emotionally unstable subjective experiences? How does a double deficit-based label enhance their well-being? What learning is taking place by disseminating deficit-based language? What you must do is change the language—which will forge new neural networks in your brain—and through repetition, strengthen these connections. Remember, that language precedes behavior. We acquire language through how we learn.

Rather than a dual diagnosis viewing two separate problems thus requiring lifelong management of each separately, it is of greater utility to view that the cognitive and emotional disturbances came first for the majority of people, especially when we know that addictive behaviors lie along a continuum. The perception is that all mental health problems are the same and they are not. This is one of the biggest problems with labeling and language. We can't look at the behaviors of individuals with severe mental illness who use drugs and alcohol and attribute them to everyone else. For example, D. J. Jaffe, the executive director of Mental Illness Policy Org, states that 20 percent of mental illness is diagnosable by the DSM and is minor consisting primarily of anxiety and depression and 4 percent represents serious mental illnesses which are not treatment resistant.[5] Therefore, to suggest that an individual who is having normal human experiences that may be seen as symptomatic of what we call depression and has learned to use addictive behaviors to cope with their life challenges should not be categorized as having a dual diagnosis.

The preconditions of addictive behaviors are chronic stress, problems in living, depressive mood states, anxiety, and the lack of effective coping skills. If your focus is only on avoiding addictive behavior and you neglect to work on other aspects of yourself, then those conditions will persist. Indeed, they'll get worse. If you're in distress, then much of what you're currently doing to compensate for your deficiencies is probably superficial. How many people do you know who say, "If I get that job, I'm going to be happy," or "When I buy that new car," "When I gain that career opportunity," "When I get married," "When I have children"? The language is always about what they lack, what they need to fill a void. This is an ineffective life strategy because it does not change your subjectivity or how you experience yourself.

By taking personal responsibility, you can deconstruct the language you have come to accept and which now dictates how you see yourself in the world. Since nobody can change your self-determining nature, your ability to learn new ways of adapting to your environment is completely in your hands. Your environment, the people and circumstances you have in your life, either helps you to grow out of early life learning experiences or helps maintain them—thus triggering and reinforcing unconscious anxieties. But studies show that even severe cases of childhood trauma, abuse, and neglect can be overcome in adulthood with the proper social support and coping skills. When you are ready and when you might want to change for your own personal reasons, make a promise to yourself to commit to the discipline of becoming more autonomous and in doing so, self-discover, acknowledge, and embrace what you fear. Initially, this is often an uncomfortable and difficult process. But it will become much easier as you begin to see positive outcomes and a renewed sense of subjective well-being. You'll become a happier person too, functioning effectively in all areas of your life. Ultimately, you already possess the motivation to do this, you now just need to access it.

13

NEW LEARNING, NEW DIRECTION

Our personal values are our convictions regarding the attitudes, beliefs, and behaviors that we consider important. They have been learned. Our values are the standards or qualities that we deem worthwhile and desirable—principles that we're committed to live by and uphold. Consistently striving to be a high-performing individual in every area of our lives is a value that everyone can benefit from, particularly those challenged with addictive behaviors. Your values will propel you toward accessing your inherent motivation to live a fulfilling life—and clearly understanding them will help you become aware of how new learning will take you into the desired new directions you choose. Nobody other than yourself can change your self-determining nature. We're all motivated to fulfill our needs. These can be biological needs, such as for food, or for housing, achievement, self-esteem, love, sex, or a variety of other things. We can also be motivated by the need for stimulation and satiation to fill an inner void or emptiness—a yearning which often leads to preoccupations and distractions. In a positive sense, we can be inspired to grow and change by changing the language we use to tell the stories about ourselves to ourselves and learning how to rewrite personal narratives. We can then plan a course of action that allows this new learning to take us in any new direction we choose.

James is a forty-five-year-old sales director applying for a new job. He also has a smoking problem. He smokes 3 packs of cigarettes a day which requires him to take too many breaks. He smokes and takes prescription pills because of chronic stress and anxiety. His potential employer has indicated to him that in spite of his significant work-related experience and qualifications that he would not seriously consider hiring him because his dependency on smoking was not in alignment with the company's health conscious core values. The employer also thought James's dependency on nicotine and medications and the amount of time wasted taking breaks throughout the workday was not the type of role model he wanted in his company. James began to rethink his values and priorities and realized he had a greater responsibility to his family as the primary source of financial support, which has contributed to his stress and anxiety. However, he now is able to associate his history of chronic stress and anxiety beginning as a teenager, as the time he began smoking.

Teri is a thirty-five-year-old marketing assistant who is quite obese and has type 2 diabetes as a result. She's recently divorced from an often unhappy marriage, and used to eat excessively because she was always depressed. Her doctor tells her she may need to be hospitalized because of her condition. Teri loves her two young children who are also obese for their age. Being a good mother is very important to her. She realizes that she is leading by example and impacting her children's lives in an unhealthy way. She begins to make the associations of past learning with its influence on her present-day thinking and behavior and decides to change by listing other areas of her life in which she's able to exercise control (her job) and uses those skills to set daily goals concerning weight loss and overall health. Teri gives herself short-term, middle-term, and long-term goals, makes drastic dietary changes, and begins an exercise regimen of walking thirty minutes daily. She also begins to educate herself on nutrition and adjusts her children's food intake accordingly.

A value-based approach to addressing addictive behaviors will empower you. They'll allow you to ask yourself the questions: "Who am I?" "What is it in my life that I should be doing?" "What responsibilities do I have to myself as well as to my family, my community, and to society?" Your acting-out behaviors are not due to a lack of control stemming from an incurable disease, but are rather a consequence of learned behavior which includes your value system or a lack thereof. For example, it's far better to refrain from stealing not because you're afraid of getting caught and arrested—rather because it's something that runs contrary to your belief about taking things that you have not paid for.

Although values are certainly necessary to preserve the social order, I'm not particularly referring to the values imposed upon you by society—but instead, to the standards by which you conduct yourself because of your desire to be the most generous representation of yourself to others and more authentic.

When your values align with your behavior, you're congruent. When you have an addictive behavior, you're incongruent: something is amiss with your values. This is why your change in behavior needs to come from inside you. But harsh self-judgments will not affect lasting change. You must reevaluate your value system—not for the purposes of conforming to what's right from wrong as dictated by society—but to empower yourself to learn new ways of dealing with your perceived and practical realities.

If you're challenged by excessive habits and addictive behaviors, you probably lack an efficient way to cope with daily problems in living, maintained by an inability to regulate emotional conflicts, poor coping skills, deficit-based habitual thinking, and misinformation about these behaviors. These are all things you've learned through life experiences. Therefore, the problems you're experiencing affect your cognition and emotions. Since labeling "addiction" as a disease is a social construct and not based on scientific evidence, part of your self-discovery will be to understand how you see yourself in relation to a system that does not view individual human experiences and personal stories as relevant to assigning a label.

As we know, the dominant ideology in addiction treatment today is based on the disease model. But to fully change thinking and improve upon your subjective experiences, it's necessary to realize that we are here on earth for a finite amount of time and we are all part of humanity. We need to understand that the world does not revolve around any one person. You can establish real values when you answer the question, "Am I living a life that matters to others?" In this reflection the objective is to not describe yourself with labels. You are a parent. You are a salesperson. You own a home. You are successful. Rather the goal is to define yourself in relation to other people. What you are is how you present yourself to others. We are separated from other animals because we have subjectivity. In communication with others we share our connection to humanity. Our values are part of this. They can provide the direction, meaning, purpose, and motivation to achieve a greater good for ourselves, our family, and our community. Our values and virtues include both attitudes and character traits, such as honesty, courage, compassion, generosity, hard work, and self-control. These are learned behaviors which we can develop through mindfulness and practice.

The problem with the way addiction is conceptualized, defined, and treated is not just because of the way conventional thinking uses "disease" and abstinence-only language, which is simply the more simplified interpretation, but rather because it's a manipulative force that covertly imposes moral righteousness. What I mean by this is that when a person surrenders to the notion that his/her normal human experiences and subsequent behaviors are deemed inappropriate we are imposing a value system. The duality of right or wrong, good or bad, all or nothing, and black or white thinking undermines and disrespects the significance of human subjective experiences.

The idea that suggests that you have to "hit bottom" before you turn things around in your life is not true. You also don't need to think that you need to wait until you've severely damaged your health, career, and family life—and then maybe you'll be willing to seek help or take it upon yourself to do something proactive. The idea of being broken down to learn life lessons is not necessary. If we only desire to help people that simply give up and lose their identity in conforming through coercive and persuasive means to share the perception of a common moral high ground, we are not helping at all.

But, it's not AA or twelve-step program's fault per se that there is so much reliance upon it. The more important question is why is it still the first—and often the only—treatment offered or available to needy individuals? Decades of research describe many positive outcomes from a variety of different approaches which attempt to change the language by not subscribing to the notions of disease and powerlessness. In fact, the evidence-based approaches encourage self-direction and empowerment as well as personal responsibility. Because of its built-in brand, AA would be better served to become secular and evolve but that would require a language change. Also, when you now consider that gambling is recognized as an addiction and looked upon in a similar way as alcohol and drugs, there are many concerns. The obvious problem is that more and more behaviors are being looked at as addictive, for example: Internet use, shopping, sex, social media use, and so on. Addictive behaviors are normal. However, if these behaviors are all labeled addictions, and addiction is called a disease, then at some point almost every pleasurable experience that you can have has the potential of being referred to as a disease. Do you really think that spending too much time on the Internet and social media is comparable to having cancer?

It's important to respect each individual's unique life experiences. If we are nicer and kinder as coaches and clinicians, and you are kinder and self-compassionate with yourself, the potential for growth and change will be greatly enhanced. We know that a self-directed effort in which people choose from options and define their own desired outcomes for themselves—will always determine a significantly greater degree of subjective well-being in the long term. What matters most to you? Your health, your physical appearance, your marriage, your children, your career, your self-respect, perhaps your social standing in the community? A life guided by clearly defined roles, responsibilities and core values makes it much easier to access your motivation to change and learn new ways to cope with your life challenges.

I find that when working with people who are experiencing challenging times, the common theme is that they're making futile attempts to get unstuck if they're using the same deficit-based language and old-school thinking that got them stuck. They establish relationships to people and things that keep them distracted and preoccupied from actually being aware that these challenges are directives that provide teaching opportunities. To produce a harmonious blend involving work, play, health, family, and community, you must have some grounding in values. Why are your values important? They influence your subjectivity. They are a part of your sense of identity, as well as giving insight into your fundamental thoughts and beliefs. They're why you do what you do.

Values also are the key to understanding your motivation. Your values reflect and influence what you want for yourself: personal satisfaction, recognition, well-being; what you want to become: individual meaning, career advancement, legacy; what you want from others: group satisfaction, integrity, connection; and what you want from society at large: broad-based meaning, culture, accountability. Knowing your values is an essential component of becoming truly self-aware. In turn, self-awareness helps you understand how people view you and allows you to identify behaviors you need to cease or modify. When you act in accord with your values and do the "right thing" for its own sake, you also reap the added bonus of self-efficacy and being a positive example for your family, friends, and coworkers. In turn, they'll often be more receptive to a principled individual who has moral credibility and engenders a high level of trust.

Since most of us have more opportunities and demands than we could ever fully satisfy, we need to carefully examine how our values connect with how we spend our time. Attention to our values helps us make ethical decisions and prioritize our goals in life. Values influence our choices—and, if we fail to align our actions with our values, over time we'll suffer the consequences of this incongruence. Failure to act in alignment with your values is a disservice to you and to others. Only constant clarification of your values will prevent this drift.

Having discovered what's really meaningful to you, it's essential that you take the next step and act on your values. The challenge then becomes resisting the stress of work and social pressures, as well as the temptations of immediate gratification that cause you to stray from what is really important to you. This is a particularly vital concern for those challenged with addictive behaviors.

What do you want in your life? What is your contribution to humanity? How can you become more empathetic? How can you become a person with a high degree of integrity? When you answer these important questions and work through a process of self-reflection you'll learn more about yourself. Self-questioning is a very powerful tool if you are honest with yourself.

Keep in mind as positive psychologist Martin Seligman suggests that motivation is always available to you if you know how to access it. His study involved 577 mildly depressed people who by all accounts lacked the motivation to change. He had them keep a daily journal in which he asked them to ask themselves what they *might* like to do and enjoy if they were not depressed. The key word being *might*.[1] After a week, follow-up of this simple exercise the people reported feeling less depressed and happier. Why? Because when you realize you can't change someone's self-determining nature you realize that ultimately the agent of change is the individual. One of the reasons the conventional treatment approaches that use deficit-based and emotionally charged language as "disease," "powerless," "denial" and "addict" usually find great resistance and in most cases avoidance is because we can't force anyone to do anything. There is natural reactance to being told what to do and why to do it. This is also because conventional approaches reinforce a dependency mindset rather than accessing the motivation to think independently and make better choices.

The opposite of dependency is autonomy. If I want to increase the likelihood of facilitating change in someone, not just their behaviors but also their thoughts and beliefs, I want to also facilitate their independence. In *Instant Influence*, Michael V. Pantalon states that reinforcing the other person's autonomy is the basis for getting them to organically change. He writes that "no one absolutely has to do anything; the choice is always yours" and "everybody already has enough motivation."[2] We need to realize that nobody can change someone's self-determining nature except the individual person, because we are motivated and make choices through the lens of our personal view of perceived and practical reality. Pantalon suggests that you don't want to make people do things for you, you want them to do it for themselves. The notions of disease and powerlessness do not reinforce autonomy—rather they reinforce dependency.

One reason why we know that a person's motivation is already available and just needs to be tapped into is seen when even the worst case problem drinkers and drug abusers still have the presence of mind to make all sorts of conscious choices in their daily lives including planning for, purchasing, and using these substances. Their brain appears to be functioning pretty well when it comes to figuring out how to get what they want. When I am asked what my coaching style is, I explain that I want to put the person I am working with in a position to succeed in all areas of his/her life through facilitating, encouraging, and supporting his/her autonomy. I believe that contrary to conventional thinking, people with addictive behavior have lost their power and they need to find it. I ask questions that give them the opportunity to have a voice.

If someone came to me and said, "I'm really depressed and I drink a lot," I would respond by saying that this was an *opportunity* to learn new things and change direction. Depending on the response, I could follow up with questions to determine the degree of how the patient perceives the seriousness of what she is experiencing, and if she wanted to, what three things might make the depression and drinking behavior subside in an effort to influence a creative response. The individuals in essence are doing their own self-assessment. Not a typical assessment to determine whether or not they meet certain criteria which is then translated into a label, rather they are having to take personal responsibility to think and rethink what's going on in their lives at that moment, including their values and motivations and what type of subjective experience they are having.

Coping skills, a solution-focused course of action, and problem-solving techniques can be implemented after a self-assessment and after the awareness of the associations of past learning experiences to the current inability to regulate emotional problems. This helps you view your own perception of reality. It's your personal narration.

Become a student of your own life. Like any successful student, you should be constantly reading, writing, thinking, and asking questions. Learning to be a critical thinker is creative. Ask yourself questions that challenge conventional thinking. For example, you're probably quite competent in some areas of your life. If you're having difficulty with a behavior that you were told you were powerless over, ask yourself, "Why is your brain still able to function to delay gratification and accomplish tasks in other areas of your life?" You now know that even the most dysfunctional drug abuser who is completely dependent physically and psychologically can make selective conscious choices that demonstrate the ability to control the behavior. You also now know that the "addicted brain"—once thought to be irreversibly damaged can actually be changed. Remember, everything you think, feel, and do changes the chemicals in your brain. So ask yourself: are my emotions and habitual thinking causing the biological changes in my brain, or are these chemicals in my brain causing my emotions and behaviors? By thinking of the mind, brain, and body as a living system, you will realize that what you think, feel, believe, and do emanates from the same source.

At some point in your life you realized that there was no Santa Claus or tooth fairy. Although these constructs gave you comfort and positive feelings, as you grew older, more educated, and more curious, you came to learn that these "characters" were not real. They did serve a purpose when you were young but you simply outgrew their usefulness since real life is reality based and these ideas from your childhood were stories and fantasy based.

Here are some things to help you think better. New learning will take you into a new direction.

1. **Self-assessment:** Don't allow yourself to be labeled. Ask yourself, "Who am I?" "What's going on in my life right now?" "Why might I be feeling stressed, depressed, anxious, frustrated, unhappy, resentful or angry?" "Why might I be telling stories to myself that I am not telling others?" You are a human being having human experiences.

2. **Fear:** We learn early on to experience as "normal" what is comfortable and familiar. You could say we fear ourselves. But fear can be a great motivator when embraced. It is a directive telling you that there is something to learn about your past experiences and the associations to your present life circumstances.

3. **Comfort:** We find comfort in discomfort. This is learned behavior and can become unlearned. If our early life experiences were filled with drama and chaos or the perception that we did not get the love, approval, and validation we were needing, we will remain stuck by similarities in future relationships with people and things.

4. **Familiarity:** We attract people and things into our lives that have been influenced by early learning experiences. We learned by "downloading" the experiences of observing and reinforcing our primary caregivers language and behavior.

5. **Relationships:** Excessive habits and addictive behaviors to anyone or anything are learned relationships used to cope with the inability to regulate emotions in healthier ways.

6. **Learning:** Early learning shapes and forms the brain's architecture and our personalities. Language precedes behavior. Behavior is learned and can be unlearned. Changing the language will change the undesired behavior.

7. **Identify triggers:** You can't solve a problem until you understand it. What's happening before you make the conscious choice to behave in a certain way? What are you thinking, feeling, and experiencing?

8. **Interrupt the behavior:** If you desire to drink, eat, or smoke, ask yourself, "Why do I want to do this right now?" Then try to immediately replace that behavior with a better choice. For example, if you desire a drink because you feel stressed and anxious, go for a long walk instead. You've learned to make the conscious choice to drink to relieve stress. Now, make the conscious

choice to exercise instead when stress is triggered. Be aware and when the feeling of depression, stress, or anxiety is upon you, try to make the association to past learning experiences.

9. **Reinforce your independence:** Take personal responsibility for your behavior. Rethink the circumstances immediately. Make associations from past experiences to the present circumstances. Change the language. You're not Bradley the alcoholic, rather Bradley who happens to be dealing with an inability to regulate his emotions and has chosen alcohol in an attempt to cope.

10. **Time management:** What do you do all day? Are you productive? How are you contributing to humanity? What's your life's direction, meaning, and purpose? Idle or self-absorbed time spent prompts rumination.

11. **Stress management:** All addictive behaviors are preceded by chronic stress, depression, and anxiety. Chronic stress impairs your autonomy, triggers fear, and inhibits new learning and rational thinking. Why might you want to find ways to reduce these feelings?

12. **Automatic thoughts:** The unconscious part of our dual track mind controls much of our behavior automatically. If your past learning experiences were marred by stress, fear, depression, and anxiety, you've learned to react to daily life situations in similar ways. By being aware of this, if you change the language, you will change the behavior. For example, "I'm a drug addict and I can't control myself" could be replaced with, "I'm consciously aware that my drug use has become a problem and that I'm unhappy and making poor coping choices, but I'm working on it."

13. **Incremental change:** Change does not need to be all or nothing, black or white. The problem drinkers who reduce drinking from ten drinks daily to five drinks daily has changed. They have also learned that they have self-control and can develop self-efficacy. Reinforce your independence, self-discover your power, have a voice, and ask yourself, "Why might I be able to handle my problematic behavior on my own?"

14. **Be self-compassionate, mindful, and empathetic:** Addictive behavior is self-indulgent.

Our self-talk and subjectivity is filled with self-criticism, self-sabotage, and self-hatred. These are learned experiences directly affected by nature and nurture. Be kind to yourself. Be kind to others. When help-seeking, look for people who are kind, compassionate, nonjudgmental, and empathetic. We are all in this world together.

AFTERWORD

At least two weekends a month Logan would be gone with his buddies, participating in highly addictive behavior. It was something that gave him a rush of euphoric feelings like nothing else ever had and he freely admitted he was hooked. His family and friends worried and became furious with him at times, calling him selfish and reckless, and accused him of having a death wish for continuing this behavior. A therapist told him his obsession with this behavior might be indicative of a type of a deeper problem and that he was not seriously considering the consequences for his behavior. But Logan replied that he just couldn't give up the feelings it gave him and he had no intention of quitting. This behavior was dangerous. Indeed, he had pushed things too far on one occasion and had to be hospitalized for a few days. When a friend of his was badly injured, Logan finally agreed that it was time to stop.

Jacob also engages in an addictive behavior with his buddies on most weekends and likewise has no intention of stopping. It makes him feel great and he freely admits he probably has a problem. He just can't seem to find any other behavior that's able to relieve his stress, makes him feel as happy, and is always there for him. His wife asks him to stop, and his parents and siblings tell him he's selfish and immature because he doesn't seem to grasp that his behavior could lead to tragic circumstances. They suggest that he be placed on medication. After a trip to the hospital upon going too far one Saturday night, Jacob finally agrees that he might have to curtail this behavior after all.

If we look at Logan and Jacob through the lens of the disease model, both men appear to have serious addictive behaviors and would be diagnosed similarly. But here's where it gets confusing. Logan is a base-jumping enthusiast. In this extreme sport, participants jump off cliffs and mountain tops and fly like a bird through the air before opening their parachute to land safely. It's very dangerous and, according to most participants, highly addictive because of the intense amount of dopamine that's released. Jacob, however, consumes prescription stim-ulant drugs daily. He also loves to use cocaine on the weekends for that dopamine rush, to relieve stress, and to have fun with his buddies as they laugh and watch sports together.

In reading these typical stories it is easy to make assumptions. But arguably each are involved in risky behaviors. Both are "addicted" to their behavior. Both continue in spite of potentially negative conse-quences. After all, there are many dangerous sports in which people occasionally die while participating. Do those individuals need rehab? Does Jacob need to stop his drug use completely, or could he learn new coping skills and deal with his stress in other ways—and maybe con-sume less?

My point here is to illustrate that people may have similar sounding or appearing problems but they are never identical, because we all experience life differently through our own subjectivity. I also wanted to highlight the concept that the reasons for, and manifestations of addictive behaviors, are specific for each individual. You must figure out for yourself the causes, conditions, and solutions as to why you're acting-out in a questionable way. Conventional thinking is like trying to put the square into the circle. The need for certainty and convenience trumps the need for autonomy, reason, and the enhancement of one's subjective experience.

So, where do we go from here? It's simple. Now is the time to take action and at your own pace. You can begin to self-direct. Never stop learning, growing, and changing. Whether you are someone who be-lieves they have a problematic behavior or someone who works with those that do, now is the time to start rethinking what you think you know. Change the language. Rethink it. Reframe it. Remove it. Allow yourself or a client or patient to tell personal stories. Listen rather than being authoritarian and thinking in absolutes. Base your success on positive outcomes from actions you initiate. Be determined to understand yourself. Do you conduct yourself with maturity, or are you immature and narcissistic? What drives you? What principles do you stand for? What are your goals and dreams? Are they organically based, or are they the product of other people's expectations? Challenge your own belief system and thought processes. Yes, doing so takes courage. But you don't have to surrender to anyone else's ideology. What you're doing now and where you're going matters more than the mistakes you've made in the past. Perhaps the most important insight of all with regard to overcoming addictive behaviors is that to achieve success you must become a more enlightened person. Read, write, and think. Otherwise you'll either continue to struggle with life distress or be confused by the conflicting ideas brought forth by the media, religious groups, and AA and twelve-step programs. One of the best ways to control addictive behaviors is to stay informed.

It is of great utility to conceptualize addictive behavior as more of a learning disorder. It's through observing others that people learn to cope with their particular life distress. Albert Bandura made us aware of observational learning: learning that occurs through observing the behavior of others. Bandura identified this basic form of learning back in the 1960s. In his experiments, children who observed their parents aggressively striking a Bobo doll would do the same thing when put in similar circumstances. This form of learning does not need reinforcement to occur, but instead, requires a model. A social model can be a parent, sibling, or teacher, but—particularly in childhood—a model is someone of authority or higher status.

Social models are important in observational learning because they help the learner encode what they observe and store it in memory for later imitation. A child may learn to swear, hit others, smoke, and do other inappropriate behaviors by the direct influence of poor modeling. Bandura discovered that children continually learn desirable and undesirable behavior through observational learning. This body of research indicates that individuals' environment, cognition, and behavior all integrate and ultimately determine how they functions later in life.[1]

For example, if as a child you watched your father become hostile and angry with your mother when discussing financial matters because he was unable to cope with the pressures of raising the family, you might respond to financial challenges as an adult in a similar way. Without having learned more appropriate coping skills you may argue with your significant other over the same issues and deal with them in the same way. It's your job to identify the learned behaviors that may be fueling problematic behaviors. It's important to understand how you learned these behaviors and choose to replace them with new positive ones and in doing so, rewire your brain, improve upon the quality of your thinking, and reinforce your autonomy.

In today's society, chronic stress is debilitating. It's embedded in the process of appraising and responding to a threatening or challenging situation—and it's triggered by your emotions, the prospect of changes taking place, family dynamics, social situations, physical pain, work challenges, fears, physical ailments, and decisions you need to make. Stress is an everyday reality. A little stress is good to keep you motivated and focused. However, too much stress can affect your memory, prevent new learning, and compromise your immune system, thereby making you susceptible to illness.

Think about yourself. First comes the life event (trigger), followed by the stress response. You biologically react. Your fight-or-flight response kicks in. Your heart races, muscles tense, blood pressure goes up. You feel out of control. Your thoughts are racing. Stress produces the release of the hormone cortisol. This chemical activity can suppress rationality and logical processes while triggering implicit memories, which are unconscious and neurologically connected to brain processes. This process leads many people to addictive behaviors in an attempt to find relief. Research has been looking at the hyperactive stress response. Through the learning principle of reinforcement, to avoid or remove the unpleasant feelings of stress, the addictive behavior becomes automatic. As daily chronic stress increases, so too does the need for the addictive behavior to reduce the stress and its unpleasant effects. We can therefore say that chronic stress plays a pivotal role as a precondition in all addictive behaviors.

Abstinence doesn't prevent trigger situations from occurring—and therefore abstinence doesn't prevent chronic stress. This is one reason why abstinence-based treatment philosophy is problematic. For many, the deficit-based language of powerlessness can contribute to feeling hopeless and helpless as well. This would make anybody chronically stressed if this was the foundation from which your subjective experiences were based on. This is also why it's not coincidental that the preconditions for excessive bad habits and addictive behaviors are chronic stress, depression, and anxiety. Rather than viewing them as co-occurring, they should be viewed as a byproduct of one's thinking. Change the language and subjectivity changes. Language changes behavior. Being mindful and self-compassionate will help one dissipate his/her biological reactivity. In doing so one gains greater self-control. Addressing underlying emotional instability and learning new coping skills to rewire the brain through specific courses of action are necessary to reframe the subjective world. This underlying emotional instability directly contributes to increasing the stress response.

I believe we are misguided in the conventional approach to addressing the problems of addictive behaviors. We spend billions of dollars on mostly ineffective drug prevention campaigns while we give lip service to the increase in prescription painkiller dependency. We attempt to solve the growing number of addictive behaviors by labeling them diseases, instead of teaching people coping skills and giving them the resources to avoid the behavior in the first place. We must rethink a system that put children as young as two years old on a stimulant drug. This is the real gateway. The gateway is the acceptance of taking drugs to correct undesirable behavior. This teaches the child, parents, teachers, doctors, and all involved in early development, that if a human experience is frowned upon by others, drugs are always a welcome remedy. We need a more balanced debate when there are new scientific findings being used to create drug policies. My best hope is to educate and empower individuals, so that they are more likely to learn how to be self-directed and autonomous in their thinking.

The disease rhetoric has been around for a long time. It's not going away. But educators need to explain the difference between a metaphoric and a literal disease. Educators need to explain social construction and the need to deconstruct the conventional language. We are approaching the tipping point in our culture when the curtain will finally be drawn on the disease model. In the preceding chapters, I've attempted to highlight the shortcomings of the prevailing mindset. I hope I've provided at least one thing that may resonate with you to help you improve upon the quality of your thinking. It is quite different to identify yourself as a human being with particular challenges rather than someone with a definitive concrete illness. That's your language choice.

With doctors and politicians on the pharmaceutical companies' payrolls, changing the language may seem futile. But with advocacy and persistence change can occur. Marijuana laws have been changing. In California nonviolent drug offenses are being reduced to misdemeanors. At the same time, rates of substance use disorders as a percentage of the population remain relatively unchanged, yet we stick with the disease model approach to treatment almost exclusively. But we can't rely solely on the government, big business, and the medical establishment to solve these problems for us. We can't expect them to do the right thing when profits and power are at stake. I don't think these problems will ever be solved from the top down. It will have to be a bottom-up movement starting with each individual.

There are alternative futures waiting for you out there—tangible and real. We absolutely can change our habitual thinking and behaviors, and render our former behavior choices a bittersweet memory of life lessons learned.

Do your best to remain committed. When you're committed there's little doubt or uncertainty; you have enthusiasm, focus, and determination. Commitment means declaring your power to manifest what you want in your life and having the courage to let go of what you say you don't. Remember, it's mostly what you think about yourself that will determine your fate. Be mindful of your environment and personal self-talk. Be aware of the stories you are telling yourself in your personal narration. Question the language you have learned to accept. Start by taking small consistent, daily positive actions that will reinforce new realities.

As a final takeaway, nothing changes without effort and a discipline in place. But since nobody can make you do anything that you don't want to do, the choices and decisions ultimately rest with you. There are no magic pills, no quick fixes, and no short-cuts. When you make the decision that experiencing more joy, happiness, and life satisfaction is something you really desire, just keep improving upon the quality of your thinking, which will affect the quality of your language, which will then affect the quality of your behavior.

NOTES

INTRODUCTION

1. Mark Pagel, *Wired for Culture: Origins of the Human Social Mind* (New York: Norton, 2013).

2. Terry Burnham and Jay Phelan, *Mean Genes: From Sex to Money to Food: Taming Our Primal Instincts* (New York: Penguin, 2001).

3. Louis Cozolino, *The Neuroscience of Psychotherapy: Building and Rebuilding the Human Brain* (New York: Norton, 2002).

4. David Levy, *Tools of Critical Thinking: Metathoughts for Psychology* (Boston: Allyn and Bacon, 1996).

5. Louis Cozolino, *The Neuroscience of Psychotherapy: Healing the Social Brain*, 2nd ed. (New York: Norton, 2010).

6. Stanton Peele, *Recover!* (Boston: Da Capo Press, 2014), 93.

7. Ellen Langer, *Power of Mindful Learning* (Boston: Da Capo Press, 1998), 4.

I. THE ORIGINS OF THE AA MINDSET

1. Ohio State Medical Society, *Transactions of the Twenty-eighth Annual Meeting*, Dayton, Ohio, 18.

2. William James, *Principles of Psychology* (Cambridge, MA: Harvard University Press, 1981), 1226. Original work published in 1890.

3. Robert D. Richardson, *William James: In the Maelstrom of American Modernism* (Boston: Houghton Mifflin, 2006), 345.

4. William James, *The Varieties of Religious Experience* (Cambridge, MA: Harvard University Press, 1985), 166. Original work published in 1902.

5. James, *Varieties of Religious Experience*, 167.

6. James, *Varieties of Religious Experience*, 157.

7. James, *Varieties of Religious Experience*, 164.

8. James, *Varieties of Religious Experience*, 171.

9. James, *Varieties of Religious Experience*, 115.

10. James, *Varieties of Religious Experience*, 384.

11. Dick B., *New Light on Alcoholism* (Kihei, HI: Paradise Research, 1999), 236.

12. Dick B., *New Light on Alcoholism*, 159.

13. Bill Wilson, *Alcoholics Anonymous Comes of Age* (New York: Author, 1957), 63.

14. Wilson, *Alcoholics Anonymous Comes of Age*.

15. Wilson, *Alcoholics Anonymous Comes of Age*, 64.

2. CHANGING OUR LANGUAGE, CHANGING OUR SUBJECTIVITY

1. Stanton Peele with Archie Brodsky, *Love and Addiction* (New York: Taplinger, 1975), Introduction.

2. Social Psychology and Personality Science, "Contextual Independence of Personality," Accessed November 24, 2014. http://www.rap.ucr.edu/navee-talSPPS.pdf.

3. Shel Silverstein, *The Missing Piece Meets the Big O* (New York: Harper and Row, 1981).

4. Nelson Mandela Quotes, Accessed October 20, 2014. http://www.goodreads.com/quotes/74396-it-is-said-that-no-one-truly-knows-a-na-tion.

3. THE REALITY OF HUMAN EXPERIENCE

1. Lance Dodes and Zachary Dodes, *The Sober Truth: Debunking the Bad Science behind 12-Step Programs and the Rehab Industry* (Boston: Beacon Press, 2014).

2. Daniel Goleman, *Vital Lies, Simple Truths: The Psychology of Self-Deception* (New York: Simon and Schuster, 1996).

3. *This Is How People Quit Addictions.* Retrieved February 5, 2015. http://www.huffingtonpost.com/stanton-peele/this-is-how-people-quit-a_b_949826.html.

4. *Journal of the American Medical Association.* "Methods Used to Quit Smoking in the United States." Accessed September 10, 2014, http://jama.jamanetwork.com/article.aspx?articleid=381957.

5. Lee N. Robins, "Vietnam Veterans' Rapid Recovery from Heroin Addiction: A Fluke or Normal Expectations?" Accessed November 4, 2014, http://www.rkp.wustl.edu/VESlit/RobinsAddiction1993.pdf.

6. Substance Abuse and Mental Health Services Administration. Accessed September 15, 2014. http://www.samhsa.gov/data/node/20

7. Albert Bandura, *Self-Efficacy: The Exercise of Control* (New York: Worth Publishers, 1997).

8. *Rise and Fall of the Official View of Addiction.* Retrieved February 5, 2015. http://www.brucekalexander.com/articles-speeches/277-rise-and-fall-of-the-official-view-of-addiction-6.

9. Bruce Alexander, *The Globalization of Addiction: A Study in Poverty of the Spirit* (New York: Oxford University Press, 2010).

4. LOVE, APPROVAL, AND VALIDATION

1. Lisa Firestone, "The Critical Inner Voice Defined." Accessed November 25, 2014. http://www.psychalive.org/the-critical-inner-voice-defined/.

2. Richard Stevens, *Erik Erikson: An Introduction* (London: Palgrave Macmillan, 1983).

3. Robert Cialdini, *Influence: The Psychology of Persuasion* (New York: HarperCollins, 2006).

4. James Holland Jones, "The Cultural Dynamics of Copycat Suicide." Accessed November 10, 2014. http://www.plosone.org/article/info%3Adoi%2F10.1371%2Fjournal.pone.0007252.

5. RETHINKING EXCESSIVE HABITS AND ADDICTIVE BEHAVIORS

1. The National Center on Addiction and Substance Abuse at Columbia University, "Addiction Medicine: Closing the Gap between Science and Practice." Accessed July 19, 2014, http://www.casacolumbia.org/addiction-research/reports/addiction-medicine.

2. Anne Fletcher, *Inside Rehab: The Surprising Truth about Addiction Treatment and How to Get Help That Works* (New York: Penguin Books, 2013).

3. Anne Fletcher, "Inside Rehab." *Psychology Today*. Accessed November 19, 2014, http://www.psychologytoday.com/blog/inside-rehab/201302/when-addiction-treatment-is-one-size-fits-all.

4. Anne Fletcher, "My Take on Celebrity Addiction-Part 2." *Psychology Today*. Accessed November 25, 2014, http://www.psychologytoday.com/blog/inside-rehab/201303/my-take-celebrity-rehabs-addiction-treatment-part-2.

5. Lance Dodes and Zachary Dodes, *The Sober Truth: Debunking the Bad Science behind 12-Step Programs and the Rehab Industry* (Boston: Beacon Press, 2014).

6. "Addiction in Women." *Harvard Health Publications*. Accessed November 12, 2014. http://www.health.harvard.edu/newsletters/Harvard_Mental_Health_Letter/2010/January/addiction-in-women.

7. *Alcoholics Anonymous* (Alcoholics Anonymous World Services, 2002).

8. Betty Grover Eisner, "Remembrances of LSD Therapy Past." Accessed May 29, 2014. http://mywordlikefire.com/tag/therapy/.

9. Mark Willenbring, "A New View of Alcoholism." *New York Times*, May 4, 2009. Accessed July 14, 2014, http://consults.blogs.nytimes.com/2009/05/04/a-new-view-of-alcoholism/?_r=0.

10. Stanton Peele, "Ten Radical Things NIAAA Research Shows about Alcoholism." http://www.peele.net/lib/niaaa.html.

11. William L. White, "The Science of Addiction Recovery: An Interview with William R. Miller, PhD, January, 2012." Accessed September 22, 2014. http://www.williamwhitepapers.com/pr/2012%20Dr.%20William%20%20Miller.pdf.

6. DECONSTRUCTING DEFICIT-BASED LANGUAGE

1. T. J. Falcone, "Alcoholism: A Disease of Speculation." Last modified November 2014. Accessed November 14, 2014. http://www.baldwinresearch.com/alcoholism.cfm.

2. Carl Hart, *High Price: A Neuroscientist's Journey of Self-Discovery That Challenges Everything You Know about Drugs and Society* (New York: HarperCollins, 2013).

3. John Tierney, "The Rational Choice of Crack Addicts," *New York Times*, September 16, 2013. Accessed November 26, 2014. http://www.nytimes.com/2013/09/17/science/the-rational-choices-of-crack-addicts.html?pagewanted=all&_r=0.

4. Nora Volkow, "Brain Imaging: Bringing Drug Abuse into Focus," National Institute on Drug Abuse. Accessed November 26, 2014. http://archives.drugabuse.gov/NIDA_Notes/NNVol18N2/DirRepVol18N2.html.

5. Gene M. Heyman, *Addiction: A Disorder of Choice* (Cambridge, MA: Harvard University Press, 2010).

6. Sally Satel and Scott O. Lilienfeld, *Brainwashed: The Seductive Appeal of Mindless Neuroscience* (New York: Basic Books, 2013).

7. Centers for Disease Control and Prevention. Last modified March 2012. Accessed May 25, 2014. http://www.nytimes.com/2013/09/17/science/the-rational-choices-of-crack-addicts.html?pagewanted=all&_r=0.

8. Celia Vimont, "Affordable Care Act to Provide Substance Abuse Treatment to Millions of New Patients." February 26, 2013. Accessed November 8, 2014. http://www.drugfree.org/join-together/affordable-care-act-to-provide-substance-abuse-treatment-to-millions-of-new-patients/.

7. PHARMACEUTICAL DRUGS AND THE DSM-5

1. Allen Frances, "Diagnosing the D.S.M.," *New York Times*, May 11, 2012. Accessed November 16, 2014, http://www.nytimes.com/2012/05/12/opinion/break-up-the-psychiatric-monopoly.html.

2. Ian Urbina, "Addiction Diagnoses May Rise under Guideline Changes," *New York Times*, May 11, 2012. Accessed November 26, 2014, http://www.nytimes.com/2012/05/12/us/dsm-revisions-may-sharply-increase-addiction-diagnoses.html?pagewanted=all.

3. CCHR International, "The DSM—Psychiatry's Billing Bible." Accessed July 8, 2014, http://www.cchrint.org/issues/dsm-billing-bible/.

4. "The DSM—Psychiatry's Billing Bible."

5. "DSM-V Task Force and Work Group Acceptance Form." Accessed November 2, 2014, http://www.dsm5.org/about/Documents/DSM%20Member%20Acceptance%20Form.pdf.

6. Allen Frances, "The New Crisis of Confidence in Psychiatric Disorders." Accessed April 19, 2014, http://annals.org/article.aspx?articleid=1722526.

7. "The DSM—Psychiatry's Billing Bible."

8. "The DSM—Psychiatry's Billing Bible."

9. "Painkiller Deaths Rise Faster in Women." July 2, 2013. Accessed October 11, 2014, http://online.wsj.com/articles/SB10001424127887324436104578581623467102896.

10. Marcia Engel, "The Epidemic of Mental Illness: Why?" *New York Review of Books*, June 23, 2011. Accessed June 15, 2014.

http://www.nybooks.com/articles/archives/2011/jun/23/epidemic-mental-ill-ness-why/.

11. "The Epidemic of Mental Illness: Why?"

12. "The Epidemic of Mental Illness: Why?"

13. "The Epidemic of Mental Illness: Why?"

8. CELEBRITY CULTURE AND ADDICTIVE BEHAVIOR

1. Alfred Adler and Colin Brett, *Understanding Human Nature* (London: Oneworld Publications, 2009).

2. Stanton Peele, "The Secret of Dr. Drew's Success," *Psychology Today*, April 13, 2011. Retrieved February 5, 2015, https://www.psychologytoday.com/blog/addiction-in-society/201104/the-secret-dr-drews-success.

3. Kory Grow, "'Glee' Rethinks Series Finale after Cory Monteith's Death," *RollingStone*, October 17, 2013. Retrieved February 5, 2014, http://www.rollingstone.com/tv/news/glee-rethinks-series-finale-after-cory-monteiths-death-20131017.

4. Stanton Peele, "Philip Seymour Hoffman Was Taught to Be Helpless before Drugs," Reason.com. February 4, 2014. Retrieved February 5, 2015, http://reason.com/archives/2014/02/04/what-the-philip-seymour-hoffman-story-te.

5. "Charlie Sheen: A Timeline of Bad Behavior," *TV Guide*, February 25, 2011, retrieved February 5, 2015, http://www.tvguide.com/news/charlie-sheen-behavior-1029895/.

6. "Lindsay Lohan Arrested for DUI, Drugs," *ABC News*, July 24, 2007. Retrieved February 5, 2015, http://abcnews.go.com/Entertainment/story?id=3408314.

7. Anahad O'Connor, "The Claim: Alcohol Kills Brain Cells," *New York Times*, November 23, 2004. Accessed November 10, 2014, http://www.nytimes.com/2004/11/23/health/23real.html?_r=0.

8. "Matthew Perry Turns Former Home into Rehab Center." Mother Nature Network, July 2, 2013. Retrieved February 5, 2015, http://www.mnn.com/health/fitness-well-being/blogs/matthew-perry-turns-former-home-into-rehab-center.

9. Peter Haldeman, "An Intervention for Malibu," *New York Times*, September 13, 2013. Accessed October 22, 2014, http://www.nytimes.com/2013/09/15/fashion/an-intervention-for-malibu.html?pagewanted=all.

9. PARENTING INFLUENCE ON CHILDREN

1. Allen Frances, "10,000 2–3 Year Old Toddlers Are on Stimulant Drugs for ADHD." *Psychology Today*, May 17, 2014. Accessed November 1, 2014, http://www.psychologytoday.com/blog/saving-normal/201405/10000-2-3-year-old-toddlers-are-stimulant-drugs-adhd.

2. "The Effects of Childhood Stress on Health across the Lifespan." Centers for Disease Control and Prevention. Accessed November 15, 2014, http://www.cdc.gov/ncipc/pub-res/pdf/Childhood_Stress.pdf.

3. Theresa Dolezal, "Hidden Costs in Healthcare: The Economic Impact of Violence and Abuse," Colorado Coalition against Sexual Assault. Accessed November 22, 2014, http://www.ccasa.org/wp-content/uploads/2014/01/Economic-Cost-of-VAW.pdf.

4. Anna Wilde Mathews, "So Young and So Many Pills." *Wall Street Journal*, December 28, 2010. Accessed August 27, 2014, http://online.wsj.com/articles/SB10001424052970203731004576046073896475588.

5. "More Teens Abusing Adderall/Ritalin-drugs in the Same Highly Addictive Class as Cocaine, Morphine and Opium." April 23, 2013. Accessed November 8, 2014, http://www.cchrint.org/2013/04/23/more-teens-abusing-adderall-ritalin/.

6. "What About Tutoring Instead of Pills?" *Der Spiegel*, August 2, 2012. Accessed February 17, 2014, http://www.spiegel.de/international/world/child-psychologist-jerome-kagan-on-overprescibing-drugs-to-children-a-847500.html.

7. Mortiz Nestor, "Inventor of ADHD's Deathbed Confession." March 27, 2013. Accessed November 7, 2014, http://www.worldpublicunion.org/2013-03-27-NEWS-inventor-of-adhd-says-adhd-is-a-fictitious-disease.html.

8. "NIH Consensus Report Highlights Controversy Surrounding ADHD Diagnosis and Stimulant Treatment." *Ethical Human Science and Services* 1(1) (1999). http://www.breggin.com/nihconsensus.pbreggin.1999.

9. "Astronomical Rise in ADHD Diagnoses Raise Questions." April 1, 2013, http://www.advisory.com/daily-briefing/2013/04/01/astronomical-rise-in-adhd-diagnoses-raises-questions.

10. "Counseling and Psychological Services Receives National Seal." Columbia University, October 28, 2013. Accessed September 15, 2014, http://sas.columbia.edu/counseling-and-psychological-services-receives-national-seal.

11. Peter R. Breggin, *Toxic Psychiatry: Why Empathy and Love Must Replace the Drugs, Electroshock, and Biochemical Theories of the New Psychiatry* (New York: St. Martin's Press, 1994).

12. Breggin, *Toxic Psychiatry*.

13. Abbe Smith, "Undue Process: Kids for Cash and the Injustice System," *New York Times*, March 29, 2013. Accessed November 15, 2014, http://www.nytimes.com/2013/03/31/books/review/kids-for-cash-and-the-injustice-system.html?pagewanted=all&_r=0.

14. Maia Szalavitz, *Help at Any Cost: How the Troubled Teen Industry Cons Parents and Hurts Kids* (New York: Riverhead Books, 2006).

15. David Dobbs, "Beautiful Brains." October 2011. Accessed November 5, 2014, http://ngm.nationalgeographic.com/print/2011/10/teenage-brains/dobbs-text.

16. Joel H. Brown, "California's Drug Education Programs Ineffective, According to Study Commissioned by the State." March–April 1997. Accessed April 18, 2014, http://ndsn.org/marapr97/cadruged.html.

17. "California's Drug Education Programs Ineffective, According to Study Commissioned by the State."

10. THE "LOVE" WE LEARNED

1. R. Chris Fraley and Philip R. Shaver, "Adult Romantic Attachment: Theoretical Developments, Emerging Controversies and Unanswered Questions," 2000. Accessed November 22, 2014, http://academic.udayton.edu/jackbauer/Readings%20595/Fraley%2000%20attch%20rev%20copy.pdf.

2. Carol G. Mooney, *Theories of Attachment: An Introduction to Bowlby, Ainsworth, Gerber, Brazelton, Kennell and Klaus* (St. Paul: Redleaf Press, 2009).

3. Deborah Blum, *Love at Goon Park: Harry Harlow and the Science of Affection* (New York: Basic Books, 2011).

4. Christopher Peterson, Steven F. Maier, and Martin E. P. Seligman, *Learned Helplessness: A Theory for the Age of Personal Control* (London: Oxford University Press, 1995).

5. "The Science of Love." BBC, September 17, 2014. Accessed October 5, 2014, http://www.bbc.co.uk/science/hottopics/love/.

6. Robert W. Firestone, *The Fantasy Bond: Structure of Psychological Defenses* (Santa Barbara, CA: Glendon Association, 1987).

7. Lisa Firestone, "How Childhood Defenses Hurt Us as Adults." *Psychology Today*, November 14, 2011. Accessed November 29, 2014, http://www.psychologytoday.com/blog/compassion-matters/201111/how-childhood-defenses-hurt-us-adults.

8. Harville Hendrix, *Getting the Love You Want* (New York: Henry Holt, 2008).

11. SUBJECTIVE WELL-BEING: THE GOAL OF ALL POSITIVE OUTCOMES

1. Edward Diener and Robert Biswas-Diener, *Happiness: Unlocking the Mysteries of Psychological Health* (Hoboken, NJ: Wiley-Blackwell, 2008).

2. Bernardo J. Carducci, *The Psychology of Personality: Viewpoints, Research and Application* (Hoboken, NJ: Wiley-Blackwell, 2009).

3. Jeanne Ellis Ormrod, *Educational Psychology: Developing Learners* (Upper Saddle River, NJ: Pearson/Merrill, 2013).

4. World Health Organization. WHO definition of Health. Accessed November 30, 2014, http://www.who.int/about/definition/en/print.html.

5. Martin Seligman, *Flourish: A Visionary New Understanding of Happiness and Well-Being* (New York: Atria Books, 2012).

6. Mihaly Csikszentmihalyi. Accessed November 30, 2014, https://www.goodreads.com/quotes/100845-repression-is-not-the-way-to-virtue-when-people-restrain.

12. RETHINKING YOUR LIFE CHALLENGES AND EXPERIENCES

1. Joseph Nowinski, "Childhood Trauma and Adult Alcohol Abuse: Shedding Light on Connection." *Huffington Post*, Updated September 21, 2013. Accessed November 12, 2014, http://www.huffingtonpost.com/joseph-nowinski-phd/alcohol-abuse_b_3595743.html.

2. Vincent J. Felitti, "The Origins of Addiction: Evidence from the Adverse Childhood Experiences Study," February 16, 2004. Accessed September 27, 2014, http://www.nijc.org/pdfs/Subject%20Matter%20Articles/Drugs%20and%20Alc/ACE%20Study%20-%20OriginsofAddiction.pdf.

3. Brain Solutions, Inc. Definition of Neuroplasticity. Accessed November 8, 2014, http://www.brainsolutionsinc.com/#!services/cy9b.

4. Jonah Lehrer, "The Reinvention of the Self." *Seed Magazine*, November 30, 2014. Accessed November 30, 2014. http://www.brainsolutionsinc.com/#!services/cy9b.

5. Peter Earley, "Against the Grain: D. J. Jaffe's 8 Myths about Mental Illness." May 16, 2014. Accessed November 12, 2014, http://www.peteearley.com/2014/05/16/against-the-grain-d-j-jaffes-8-myths-about-mental-illness/.

13. NEW LEARNING, NEW DIRECTION

1. Michael V. Pantalon, *Instant Influence* (New York: Little, Brown, 2011), 30.

2. Pantalon, *Instant Influence*, 25.

AFTERWORD

1. Albert Bandura, *Psychological Modeling: Conflicting Theories* (Chicago: Aldine Transaction, 2006).

GLOSSARY

Addictive behavior This is an expression of a person's self-determining nature. It is a learned behavior exhibited by an individual to cope with life's challenges based upon the subjective perception of reality.

Adverse childhood experiences (ACE) Extremely negative childhood experiences such as abuse or trauma.

Alcoholics Anonymous (AA) Founded in 1935 by stockbroker Bill Wilson and physician Robert Smith, it remains the most important organization in the world aiding alcohol dependency. It stresses the "disease concept" of alcohol dependency and individual powerlessness before a higher power. Members regularly attend group meetings and gain an individual sponsor to achieve sobriety.

Attachment Theory Based significantly upon the work of psychologist Mary Ainsworth, it emphasizes that the quality of the relationship between adult caretaker (typically the biological mother) and infant/toddler has lifelong impact on the child's ability to form intimacy with others.

Attention Deficit Hyperactivity Disorder (ADHD) A biological condition usually diagnosed in childhood involving both attentional deficits and hyperactive behavior. Daily medication is typically part of the treatment regimen to control these problems but does not cure the condition.

Big Book, The   Originally published in 1939, it was written by Bill Wilson and Robert Smith and has been the basic text or "bible" of AA ever since.

Classical conditioning   The learning paradigm formulated by early behaviorists in which a conditioned stimulus like the sound of a bell is paired with an unconditioned stimulus like the odor of cooked meat to elicit an initially unconditioned response like canine salivation, which then becomes a conditioned response.

Cognitive dissonance   A psychological term originated by Leon Festinger to describe the confusion that people feel when faced with information that contradicts a strongly held belief.

Deficit-based language   Words and phrases that are emotionally charged and have a negative connotation such as "disease," "powerless," "drug addict," "alcoholic," "addiction," and "clean."

Developmental Stage Theory   A theory of human personality, such as advanced by Erik Erikson and Sigmund Freud, that associates specific periods of life, such as infancy, toddlerhood, or adolescence, with particular psychological gains and challenges.

Disease model of addiction   It defines alcohol and drug dependency as a biologically based condition, involving the brain and neurological system, and that require lifelong treatment.

Dislocation Theory   The theory that addictive behaviors arise when people lack psychosocial integration. The breakdown of the family and globalization have made people more disconnected from themselves and others. This situation is seen to create stress, anxiety, depression, and other preconditions leading to addictive behavior as a means to cope.

Dopamine   A neurotransmitter that helps control the brain's reward and pleasure centers but also involved in learning and memory.

Dual diagnosis   In the mental health field, this term refers to individuals who have two distinct psychiatric disorders, such as depression and alcohol dependency. This situation is known as co-morbidity.

Dual-track mind   This is the psychological concept that human cognition typically comprises a conscious flow of thought coupled with self-awareness combined with unconscious thoughts (that is, below usual awareness).

Empathy   The ability to relate to the feelings of others. Psychologists today differentiate between the cognitive and affective components of empathy; that is, knowing intellectually what someone is feeling and being able to experience those feelings.

Fantasy bond   A form of self-protection seen in relationships in which there is an illusion of real connection with another person. Such self-protection begins developing as a consequence of painful early childhood experiences.

Flow experiences   First described by the Czech psychologist Mihali Csikzentmihaly, these are positive experiences of "being in the zone" encompassing complete concentration on the task at hand, a loss of self-consciousness, and enjoyment of the experience for its own sake.

Inner child   A psychologist concept that emerged from addiction treatment in the 1980s and popularized by Charles Whitfield, it affirms that within the healthy adult personality are positive traits like playfulness and spontaneity that originate in healthy childhood development.

Interpersonal biology   The scientific discipline that seeks to bridge the gap between the biological and social sciences. Its goal is to understand how human relationships interact with the brain to shape and form mental life.

Learned Helplessness Theory   A psychological term developed by Martin Seligman based on his experiments with dogs and generalized to "real-life" human situations. It refers to a situation when an organism believes it is powerless to alter conditions that give it rewards or punishments and therefore ceases to act differentially in response to stimuli.

Locus of control   A psychological term developed by Julian Rotter to describe if a person views oneself as controlling or directing of his/her life or instead as being passively controlled or directed by others.

Mindfulness   A psychologist concept first developed by Jon Kabat-Zinn based on Buddhist meditation and generalized to many types of relaxation training and stress management. The emphasis is on focusing one's attention fully in the present moment to reap mental and physical benefits.

Mindlessness   The opposite of mindfulness. Losing or abandoning the ability to remain focused mentally on the present moment, and instead diverting to fixating mentally on the past or worrying about the future.

Motivational style   A psychological term describing a person's particular or main focus on goals. Intrinsic motivation refers to inner-directed goals, such as self-fulfillment. Extrinsic motivation refers to outer-directed goals, such as money or social status.

Nadir experience   A psychological term coined by Abraham Maslow to describe an emotionally painful, "dark-night-of-the-soul" experience, that ultimately leads to personality growth. In AA and twelve-step program parlance, this is often referred to as "hitting rock bottom."

Narcissism   A psychologist concept originating with Sigmund Freud and developed significantly by Heinz Kohut, an Austrian-born American psychoanalyst, as a specific type of personality disorder. The individuals have an inflated sense of their own importance coupled with an inability to value others adequately.

Neuroplasticity   The scientific finding that the human brain can change throughout the individual's life as a result of experience. Every time one practices an old skill or learns a new one, existing neural connections are strengthened, and over time, neurons create more connections. Even new nerve cells are generated.

Object Relations Theory   Developed from Freudian theory by Melanie Klein and amplified mainly by British psychoanalysts, it emphasizes how the human infant processes reality to develop a sense of self.

Observational learning   A psychological concept originally developed by Alfred Bandura based on experiments involving children. It emphasizes that individuals can learn new behaviors simply by watching others, such as when young children learn by observing their parents' behaviors.

Obsessive Compulsive Disorder (OCD)   A psychiatric disorder characterized by either obsessions (unwanted, disturbing, and intrusive thoughts) or compulsions (repetitive behaviors and mental acts). Hoarding behavior has recently been viewed as a manifestation of this disorder.

Parenting style   A psychological concept originally developed by Diana Baumrind. It analyzes the methods that parents use in their child-rearing. Four main methods have been identified: authoritarian, indulgent, authoritative, and neglectful.

Resilience   A major concept in positive psychology, it refers to the ability of an individual to "bounce back" from stress into his/her previous (presumably normal or healthy) state of psychological well-being.

Self-compassion   A recent concept in positive psychology that emphasizes the importance of treating oneself gently and kindly. People raised in dysfunctional families often lack this trait in their daily lives.

Self-determining   The actual ongoing choices and decisions an individual makes in order to live their lives in the way they have learned to accept.

Self-efficacy   A relatively recent psychological concept developed by Albert Bandura. It refers to the individual's confidence in the ability to cope well with life's stresses and challenges.

Self-esteem   A psychological concept, developed by Nathaniel Branden and popularized in American culture during the 1970s, that refers to individuals' overall evaluation of their own worth.

Serotonin   A neurotransmitter primarily found in the gastrointestinal tract, platelets, and the central nervous system of animals, including humans. It is popularly thought to be a contributor to feelings of well-being and happiness.

Sexual addiction   A term developed in the addiction field to describe as an intimacy disorder characterized by compulsive sexual thoughts and acts. Despite the promulgation of treatment programs and rehab centers for this condition, recent scientific research has questioned whether it actually resembles alcohol and drug dependencies.

Social anxiety disorder   A psychiatric disorder in which the individual experiences severe stress in the presence of other people, even in commonplace group situations, such as a college classroom or movie theater.

Social learning theory   Developed by Albert Bandura, it posits that people learn from another via observation, imitation, and modeling. The theory has often been called a bridge between behaviorist and cognitive learning theories because it encompasses attention, memory, and motivation.

Social proof   Also known as informational social influence. It refers to the positive influence created by seeing other people do something. The individual therefore believes that the behavior must therefore be the right or proper thing to do.

Solution-focused therapy (SFT)   It is a goal-directed approach to psychotherapeutic change that is conducted through directly observing the client's responses to a series of precisely constructed questions. There is minimal focus on the client's past.

Subjective experience The moment by moment experiences of living one's life cognitively and emotionally unique to each individual.

Subjectivity The way an individual frames their perceived and practical reality through the quality of their thinking.

Subjective well-being A major concept in positive psychology, it refers to an individual's usual level of happiness. Ed Diener has been a leading researcher in this field.

Twelve-Step Programs Based on the AA approach to alcohol dependency, such programs now encompass a variety of addictive behaviors, such as gambling and overeating.

Value-based approach to addictive behaviors This approach derives from humanistic psychology including the theories of Abraham Maslow and Rollo May. It emphasizes the role of personal values in addictive behaviors such as alcoholism and drug abuse.

BIBLIOGRAPHY

ABC News. "Lindsay Lohan Arrested for DUI, Drugs." July 24, 2007. http://abc-news.go.com/Entertainment/story?id=3408314.

Adler, Alfred, and Colin Brett. *Understanding Human Nature: The Psychology of Personality*. London: Oneworld Publications, 2009. (Originally published in 1927.)

Alcoholics Anonymous. *The Big Book*. Akron, OH: AA World Services, 1939.

American Psychiatric Association. *DSM-V. American Psychiatric Association*. http://www.psychiatry.org.

Angell, Marcia. "The Epidemic of Mental Illness: Why?" *New York Review of Books*, June 23, 2011.

Bandura, Albert. *Self-Efficacy: The Exercise of Control*. New York: Freeman, 1997.

———. *Psychological Modeling: Conflicting Theories*. Piscataway, NJ: Aldine Transaction, 2010.

Blum, Deborah. *Love at Goon Park: Harry Harlow and the Science of Affection*. New York: Basic Books, 2002.

Breggin, Peter R. *Toxic Psychiatry: Why Empathy and Love Must Replace the Drugs, Electroshock, and Biochemical Theories of the New Psychiatry*. New York: St. Martin's Press, 1991.

Brown, Joel H. "California's Drug Education Programs Ineffective." www.ndsn.org/ma-rapr97, April 1997.

Burnham, Terry, and Jay Phelan. *Mean Genes: From Sex to Money to Food*. New York: Penguin, 2001.

Carducci, Bernardo J. *The Psychology of Personality: Viewpoints, Research and Applications*. Edison, NJ: Wiley-Blackwell, 2009.

Carlat, Daniel. *Unhinged: The Trouble with Psychiatry: A Doctor's Revelations of a Profession in Crisis*. New York: Free Press, 2010.

Centers for Disease Control and Prevention. http://www.cdc.gov/tobacco/data_statistics Centers for Disease Control and Prevention. "Policy Impact: Prescription Painkiller Overdoses." http://www.cdc.gov.

Centers for Disease Control and Prevention. "Adverse Childhood Experiences Study (ACE)." http://www.cdc.gov/ace.

Cialdini, Robert. *Influence: Science and Practice*. New York: HarperCollins, 1993.

Cornwall, Michael. *Ten Examples of Classical Conditioning*. North Charleston, SC: CreateSpace, 2011.

Cosgrove, Lisa. "Diagnosing Conflict of Interest Disorder." American Association of University Professors. http://www.aaup.org, December 2013.

Cosgrove, Lisa, and Krimsky, Sheldon. "Financial Associations with Industry." http://www.ethics.harvard.edu.

Cozolino, Louis. *The Neuroscience of Psychotherapy: Building and Rebuilding the Human Brain.* New York: Norton, 2002.

———. *The Neuroscience of Psychotherapy: Healing the Social Brain.* 2nd ed. New York: Norton, 2010.

Dick, B. *New Light on Alcoholism: God, Sam Shoemaker, and A.A.* Kihei, HI: Paradise Research, 1999.

Diener, Ed, and Robert Biswas-Diener. *Happiness: Unlocking the Mysteries of Psychological Wealth.* Edison, NJ: Wiley-Blackwell Publishing, 2008.

Dobbs, David. "Beautiful Brains." *National Geographic Magazine,* October 2011.

Dolezal, Theresa. "Hidden Costs in Healthcare: The Economic Impact of Violence and Abuse." http://www.partnerforviolenceprevention.org.

Drug Enforcement Administration. "Drug Schedule II." http://www.justice.gov/dea/druginfo.

Eisner, Betty Grover. "Remembrances of LSD Therapy Past." http://www.mywordlikefire.com

Falcone, T. J. *Alcoholism: A Disease of Speculation.* Amsterdam, NY: Baldwin Research Institute, 2003.

Felitti, Vincent J. "The Origins of Addiction: Evidence from the Adverse Childhood Experiences Study." Department of Preventive Medicine, Kaiser Permanente Medical Care Program, San Diego, California. http://www.acestudy.org/files/originsofaddiction.pdf, 2004.

Fingarette, Herbert. *Heavy Drinking: The Myth of Alcoholism as a Disease.* Berkeley: University of California Press, 1988.

Firestone, Lisa. "How Childhood Defenses Hurt Us as Adults," *Psychology Today,* November 14, 2011.

Firestone, Robert W. *The Fantasy Bond: Structure of Psychological Defenses.* Santa Barbara, CA: Glendon Association, 1985.

Fraley, C., and P. Shaver. "Adult Romantic Attachment: Theoretical Developments, Emerging Controversies and Unanswered Questions." *Review of General Psychology* 4, no. 2 (2000): 132–54.

Frances, Allen J. "Diagnosing the DSM." *New York Times,* May 11, 2013.

Goleman, Daniel. *Vital Lies, Simple Truths: The Psychology of Self-Deception.* New York: Simon & Schuster, 1996.

Gregoire, Thomas. "Alcoholism: The Quest for Transcendence and Meaning." *Clinical Social Work Journal* 23, no. 10 (1995): 339–59.

Grow, Kory. RollingStone. "'Glee' Rethinks Series Finales after Cory Monteith's Death." October 17, 2013. http://www.rollingstone.com/tv/news/glee-rethinks-series-finale-after-cory-monteiths-death-20131017

Haldeman, Peter. "An Intervention for Malibu," *New York Times,* September 13, 2013.

Hart, Carl. *High Price: A Neuroscientist's Journey of Self-Discovery That Challenges Everything You Know about Drugs and Society.* New York: HarperCollins, 2013.

Harvard Health Publications. "Addiction in Women." http://www.health.harvard.edu, January 2010.

Hendrix, Harville. *Getting the Love You Want: A Guide for Couples.* New York: Henry Holt, 2001.

Heyman, Gene M. *Addiction: A Disorder of Choice.* Cambridge, MA: Harvard University Press, 2009.

JED Foundation Press Release. http://www.jedfoundation.org, June 11, 2013.

James, William. *Principles of Psychology.* Cambridge, MA: Harvard University Press, 1980. (Original work published 1890.)

———. *Varieties of Religious Experience.* Cambridge, MA: Harvard University Press, 1985. (Original work published 1902.)

Jellinek, Elivin M. "Phases of Alcohol Addiction." *Quarterly Journal of Studies of Alcohol* 13, no. 13 (1952): 673–84.

————. *The Disease Concept of Alcoholism.* New Brunswick, NJ: Hillhouse Press, 1960.

Kagan, Jerome. "What about Tutoring Instead of Pills?" http://www.spiegel.de.

Kirsch, Irving. *The Emperor's New Drugs: Exploding the Antidepressant Myth.* New York: Perseus, 2010.

Langer, Ellen. *Power of Mindful Learning.* Boston: Da Capo, 1997.

Levy, David. *Tools of Critical Thinking: Metathoughts for Psychology.* Boston: Allyn and Bacon, 1996.

Martin, Clancy. "Addiction Nation." *Elle Magazine,* July 2013.

Maslow, Abraham H. *Toward a Psychology of Being* (2nd ed.). Princeton, NJ: Van Nostrand, 1968.

————. *Religions, Values, and Peak Experiences.* New York, NY: Viking, 1970.

————. *Motivation and Personality.* 3rd ed. White Plains, NY: Wilder Publications, 1987.

Mathews, Anne Wilde. "So Young and So Many Pills," *Wall Street Journal,* December 28, 2010.

Mental Health Watchdog. http:// www.cchrint.org/issues.

Mesoudi, Alex. "The Cultural Dynamics of Copycat Suicide." *PLOS One* 4 no. 9, e 7252.

Miller, W. R., and R. F. Munoz. *Controlling Your Drinking: Tools to Make Moderation Work for You.* New York: Guilford, 2004.

Mooney, Carol G. *Theories of Attachment: An Introduction to Bowlby, Ainsworth, Gerber, Brazelton, Kennell and Klaus.* St. Paul, MN: Redleaf Press, 2009.

Mother Nature Network. "Matthew Perry Turns Former Home into Rehab Center." July 2, 2013. http://www.mnn.com/health/fitness-well-being/blogs/matthew-perry-turns-former-home-into-rehab-center

National Center on Addiction and Substance Abuse at Columbia University. "Addiction Medicine: Closing the Gap between Science and Practice." New York: 2012.

National Institute on Alcohol Abuse and Alcoholism (NIAAA). *National Longitudinal Alcohol Epidemiologic Survey (NLAES)* (1998).

Nestor, Moritz; "Inventor of ADHD's Deathbed Confession." http://www.worldpublicunion.org, March 27, 2013.

O'Connor, Anahad. "The Claim: Alcohol Kills Brain Cells," *New York Times,* November 23, 2004.

Ohio State Medical Society. *Transactions of the Twenty-eighth Annual Meeting.* Dayton, OH: United Brethren, 1873.

Ormrod, J. E. *Educational Psychology: Developing Learners.* 7th ed. Upper Saddle River, NJ: Pearson, 2010.

Pascual-Leone, A., Amir Amedi, F. Fregni, and L. B. Merabet. "The Plastic Human Brain Cortex." *Annual Review of Neuroscience* 28 (2005): 377–401.

Pagel, Mark. *Wired for Culture: Origins of the Human Social Mind.* New York: Norton, 2013.

Peele, Stanton, with Archie Brodsky. *Love and Addiction.* New York: Taplinger, 1975.

Peele, Stanton. *Recover!* Boston: Da Capo, 2014.

————. "The Secret of Dr. Drew's Success," *Psychology Today,* April 13, 2011. https://www.psychologytoday.com/blog/addiction-in-society/201104/the-secret-dr-drews-success

————. Reason.com, "Philp Seymour Hoffman Was Taught to Be Helpless before Drugs," February 4, 2014. http://reason.com/archives/2014/02/04/what-the-philip-seymour-hoffman-story-te

Peterson, Christopher, Stephen F. Maier, and Martin E. P. Seligman. *Learned Helplessness: A Theory for the Age of Personal Control:* Oxford: Oxford University Press, 1995.

"Psychiatrist Now Admits He Helped Invent ADHD." http://www.childrens behaviorproblems.com/psychiatrist.

Rakic, P. "Neurogenesis in Adult Primate Neocortex: An Evaluation of Evidence." *Nature Reviews Neuroscience* 3 (2005): 65–71.

Richardson, Robert D. *William James: In the Maelstrom of American Modernism.* Boston: Houghton Mifflin, 2006.

Satel, Sally, and Scott O. Lilienfeld. *Brainwashed: The Seductive Appeal of Mindless Neuroscience.* New York: Basic Books, 2013.

Schwartz, J. M., Henry P. Stapp, and M. Beauregard. "The Volitional Influence of the Mind on the Brain, with Special Reference to Emotional Self-Regulation." In *Consciousness, Emotional Self-Regulation and the Brain*. Edited by Mario Beauregard. Amsterdam, Netherlands: John Benjamins, 2004.

Seligman, Martin E. P. *Flourish: A Visionary New Understanding of Happiness and Well-Being*. New York: Free Press, 2011.

"The Science of Love." http://www.bbc.co.uk/science/hottopics/love.

Silverstein, Shel. *The Missing Piece Meets the Big O*. New York: Harper and Row, 1981.

Smith, Abbe. "Undue Process: 'Kids for Cash' and 'the Injustice System,'" *New York Times*, March 29, 2013.

Stevens, Richard. *Erik Erikson: An Introduction*. New York: Palgrave Macmillan, 1983.

Szalavitz, Maia. *Help at Any Cost: How the Troubled-Teen Industry Cons Parents and Hurts Kids*. New York: Riverhead, 2006.

"Thinker of the Year Award—2000, Milhaly Csikszentmihalyi." http://www.brainchannels.com/thinker/mihaly.

Tierney, John. "The Rational Choice of Crack Addicts." *New York Times*, September 16, 2013.

TV Guide. "Charlie Sheen: A Timeline of Bad Behavior," February 25, 2011. http://www.tvguide.com/news/charlie-sheen-behavior-1029895/

U.S. Food and Drug Administration. http:// www.fda.org/drugs.

U.S. National Survey on Drug Use and Health. http://www.samhas.gov/data/nsduh/2k8nsduh.

Volkow, Nora D. "Brain Imaging: Bringing Drug Abuse into Focus." *National Institute on Drug Abuse Notes* 18, no. 2 (2003).

Walle, Alf. "William James' Legacy to Alcoholics Anonymous: An Analysis and a Critique." *Journal of Addictive Diseases* 11, no. 3 (1992): 91–99.

Whitaker, Robert J. *Anatomy of an Epidemic: Magic Bullets, Psychiatric Drugs and the Astonishing Rise of Mental Illness*. New York: Crown, 2010.

Willenbring, Mark. "A New View of Alcoholism," *New York Times*, May 4, 2009.

Wilson, Bill. *Alcoholics Anonymous Comes of Age*. New York: Author, 1957.

INDEX OF TERMS

INDEX OF NAMES